the LIVEBAIT
cookbook

the LIVEBAIT cookbook

Rambunctious Seafood Cooking

Theodore Kyriakou

and

Charles Campion

SOMA
san francisco

First published in Great Britain in 1998 by Hodder & Stoughton, London. North American edition published 1998 by SOMA Books, by arrangement with Hodder & Stoughton

SOMA Books is an imprint of Bay Books & Tapes, Inc., 555 De Haro St., No. 220, San Francisco, CA 94107

Design: Isobel Gillian
Photography and styling: Sandra Lane

For the SOMA edition:
Publisher: James Connolly
North American Editor: Peter Garnham

ISBN 1-57959-027-6

Printed in Hong Kong
10 9 8 7 6 5 4 3 2 1
Distributed by Publishers Group West

Library of Congress Cataloging-in-Publication Data
Kyriakou, Theodore
    The Livebait Cookbook / Theodore Kyriakou and Charles Campion
        p.   cm.
    Includes index
    ISBN 1-57959-027-6 (hc : cloth : alk. paper)
    1. Cookery (Seafood) 2. Livebait (Restaurant)   I. Campion,
Charles.   II. Title.
TX747.K97   1998
641.6'92--dc21   98-27870
                                                    CIP

A Word of Thanks

It is only when you come to write a paragraph that thanks everyone for their help that you find out just what a team game writing cookbooks can be. With an apology in advance to all those who we have inadvertently omitted ....

Thanks are due to the brigade in the Livebait Covent Garden kitchen, particularly Bridget Chick, Beatrice Ferrante, Yannick Tual, Michaela Beer, Matthew Laine, James Enrile, Alexander Carvajal, Patrick Jamleck Kiragu, Eric Mulundi, and Nick Brown for bearing up despite a lot more filleting, cooking, and preparation work. Also to the managers and front-of-house staff: Paloma Santa Maria, Linda Miles, Justine Mclennan, Deborah Fellows, Emma Clyde, Lisa Stephenson, Sharon Fennell, and Carlo Renzulli, for running a restaurant despite having someone writing in one corner, someone taking photographs in another, and all of it happening at lunch time! Also Mark Yates and Katrin Olander, without whom there would never have been a Livebait in the first place, and to Neville Abraham and Laurence Isaacson, whose restaurant company Groupe Chez Gérard not only bought the original Livebait restaurant at Waterloo but had enough faith in the concept to create the new and large Livebait in Covent Garden. To Manu Feidel, Emma Scott, and the team at Livebait Waterloo. To Susan Campbell, for tirelessly testing an endless succession of fish recipes, (usually against the clock). To Clayre Broadfield, for testing some of the other recipes. To Roland Philipps, Anna-Maria Watters, and Hazel Orme at Hodder and Stoughton for putting up with weeks of, "We'll be sending you some more manuscript soon." Also to Isobel Gillan for laying out the book so elegantly, and Sandra Lane for her exceptional photographs. And, finally, to all the fish-loving customers who have made Livebait such a success.

Theodore Kyriakou and Charles Campion,
Livebait Covent Garden August 1998

Contents

A surprise around every corner

Charles Campion

My first visit to Livebait (which in those days was a small black and white tiled establishment, in a street named The Cut behind Waterloo Station) was a strange one. For a start it was four o'clock in the afternoon, and for another thing I was in the middle of a day-long oyster-eating marathon (one of the more enjoyable surveys I have undertaken for *ES*, the Friday magazine of the London *Evening Standard*). I reached Livebait with the first four dozen oysters under my belt, quite literally. As I walked in, Theodore looked me up and down and came out of the kitchen with a large basket of bread and a pint of Guinness. The bread was amazing: there was a yellow-hearted loaf musty with turmeric, a dark one with flecks of olive, one bright red with smoky paprika – all were warm, all were delicious. Particularly to a passer-by who had spent the day sampling mollusks and so ingesting about a gallon of cold sea water. The oysters were good too, lovingly opened, carefully presented. So this was it, the fish restaurant everyone was talking about.

Then, as now, the Livebait speciality seemed to be an ability to cause the maximum amount of stir in the minimum amount of time. Livebait first opened its doors on September 26, 1995: the restaurant was a partnership between the chef Theodore Kyriakou, and Mark Yates and his fiancée, Katrin Olander, who were responsible for the front-of-house. There were also two "sleeping partners," Michael Wood and Mick Richards. The venture was a brave one by all concerned and had a good deal more enthusiasm behind it than hard cash – one of the reasons for the "minimalist" design of the banquettes and the simple black and white tiling is that the partners built the seating and did all the initial painting and decorating themselves. Anything much more complicated would probably have proved too costly.

Throughout the latter part of the 1990s any, and every, chic London restaurant would proudly allude to its philosophy; some even boasted written "mission statements." They all felt the need for a precise description of their food – "Modern British," vying with "Pacific Rim," "Mediterranean," or "Fusion." Livebait has had no such formal straitjacket, but it has nurtured its own distinctive philosophy. What Theodore and his team have created is the ultimate in "market-driven" restaurants: in Waterloo – and now in Covent Garden – the menu at Livebait changes daily, not in response to the latest fashions, not even in response to the whims of the head chef, but in response to the market. Having set out to buy only the best fish, who can tell what will be best later on in the week? Today there is a huge and beautifully fresh turbot, tomorrow (if most of today's customers are sensible enough to choose the turbot dish from

the menu) there will be no turbot to be had. The menu is constantly changing and always exciting, and Livebait regulars find themselves choosing confidently – exotic fish, innovative combinations, even dishes they have never heard of.

As any French chef will tell you (indeed, it is a subject any French chef will be delighted to lecture you on), British diners love the plain and unadventurous; lack discernment; and are hell to cook for. Then, reluctantly, Monsieur will go on to tell you that things in Britain "may be getting a little better." Livebait is one of the places where this improvement is most marked. In a country where fish is still viewed with suspicion, it is amazing to think that a restaurant can succeed by offering roast cod with butter bean and black pudding stew; or by serving nearly raw seared tuna; or by teaming monkfish and belly pork. Hurrah for the customers! The result of this open-mindedness has been a niche for Livebait, and acclaim as the most consistently innovative fish restaurant in Britain. It also means exciting dining. You might compare it to watching the final stages of a village cricket match: the blacksmith swings wholeheartedly at every ball. Mostly he connects and the ball vanishes into the next parish, but occasionally he misses whereupon he is out. The important thing is that it is always exciting and never dull – the perfect summary of everything that is best about dining at Livebait.

As word of these strange combinations of fish and meat, or fish and shellfish, or simply of unheard-of exotic fish, started to leak out, London's restaurant critics – after the usual period spent squabbling over who was first to discover the place – gave Livebait better and better reviews. Awards followed, and by February 1997 Groupe Chez Gérard, a large restaurant company, stepped in with an offer to buy. (As Victor Kiam is so fond of saying in his television ads, they "liked the product so much they bought the company!") For Neville Abraham and Laurence Isaacson of Groupe Chez Gérard, the Livebait concept represented something new and vital, and what was even more exciting it specialized in fish. Livebait made the perfect counterweight to their highly successful Chez Gérard chain which is renowned for paying homage to steak frîtes.

The challenge for Theodore Kyriakou was to take his personal and highly idiosyncratic style of cooking and make it work in a brand-new, larger restaurant over the river in Covent Garden. Theodore was born in Athens, where his parents ran a prosperous delicatessen and food shop. Some of his earliest memories are of long ferry trips with his father to purchase olives from producers scattered throughout the Greek islands. Or of making the yearly visit to buy the grapes, which were then to be shipped back to Athens to make wine for the family. For someone with such an early grounding in good food, it took him a surprisingly long time to find his way to a career in the kitchen.

Theodore left school for college to study for his exams in the Merchant Navy, and then for many years he criss-crossed the world's oceans as he worked his way up from third officer to second captain. After a couple of spells low on income but high on adrenaline, when he volunteered his services for successive Greenpeace missions, he found himself in London looking around for a new career. Necessity meant that the kitchen finally beckoned. In 1988 he started working as a *commis* chef at Pollyanna's on Battersea Rise, London; by 1993 he had done stints as *chef de partie* under Dan Evans at the Fire Station restaurant in Waterloo, London, and with Fergus Henderson at St John in Clerkenwell, London. In 1994 he got his first job as a head chef at the Stepping Stone restaurant, Battersea Rise, London. A year later he had opened Livebait. A fairly meteoric assault, by any standards, upon what has recently become a competitive and glamorous profession.

For the opening of the second Livebait in Covent Garden, Theodore made the unusual decision to start with completely new kitchen staff, rather than leave the original restaurant with a parallel problem by moving his old brigade across the river. His problems were compounded by the arrangement of the kitchens at Wellington Street. The restaurant is within the building that houses the Lyceum theater and a good many facilities must be shared. The main kitchen is deep within the theater and is linked by elevator to a small open service kitchen at one end of the restaurant. The day's work starts down in the main kitchen with all the preparation and then, just before the lunch rush starts, all the chefs troop upstairs to man the service kitchen where the dishes are cooked and finished. The same procedure is repeated each evening. Living cheek by jowl with the theater has led to some amusing incidents, especially in the early days. Amid the flurry of opening parties and while working out how to get the best from various bits of new machinery, even the most saintly chefs can find their tempers fraying, and so it was that a message was bellowed down the intercom to a French kitchen porter – let's call him Pierre. "Bring up the large cod, immediately" would give the meaning of his instructions, though not convey the vocabulary or urgency with which they were issued. Pierre duly snatched up a handsome 6-pound cod and bolted out of the kitchen for the restaurant. But instead of turning left

up the stairs, he turned right through the swing doors deeper into the theater, then the one-way doors promptly swung shut behind him. On he wandered until eventually he found himself backstage during a performance of *Jesus Christ Superstar*. By this time what little English he could speak had quite deserted him, leaving the theater's front-of-house manager to telephone the restaurant and ask, "Have you lost a small Frenchman with a large fish?"

There was also the unfortunate occasion when ghostly music could be heard during every lull in the performance. This was finally traced back to a chef's radio, which was echoing in the shaft of the food elevator where it had been used as a makeshift doorstop.

When enthusing about the new Livebait restaurant during a television interview Laurence Isaacson said, "We wanted it to be a more accessible kind of fish restaurant, where you can sit at the bar and enjoy a bottle of beer and half a dozen oysters, just as much as settling down to an elaborate three-course dinner." And that's what Livebait has become; perhaps its greatest strength is that it is completely classless. Stylish, yes. Snobbish, no. Just like Theodore's recipes.

Most cooks would concede that they don't make as much use of fish as perhaps they should. We know that fish is good for us, but we're still scared of the bones and wedded to soggy fillets in batter. We are all guilty of underestimating and overlooking fish, despite knowing in our heart of hearts that it is a splendid natural food.

Diners at Livebait will tell you that fish can be made exciting, and Theodore's recipes will show you that exciting fish dishes are a lot easier than you think. Enjoy this book (in the process eat a good deal more fish) – and you'll find there's a surprise around every corner.

surprise

Fish tales – an early-morning stroll through Billingsgate fish market

C.C. *There's no doubt about it, 4.30 A.M. is very early indeed, but the market is just beginning to buzz. Are you a regular visitor to Billingsgate?*

T.K. To tell you the truth, I have never been before. At Livebait we are always trying to work our way back up the supply chain, because that means fresher fish and a better choice. Rather than buy from a wholesaler – who buys from a Billingsgate dealer, who in turn buys from a trawler's agent – we like to buy direct from the boat. It can mean that we get our fish as much as forty-eight hours fresher. Of course, all the overseas and exotic fish comes in by air freight, but for these we try to deal with the shipper rather than the wholesaler whenever possible. Most of our inshore fish comes up from Poole harbour in Dorset, and we also get a lot from Guernsey – the waters are very clean around the Channel Islands.

So as Billingsgate is new to you, what are your first impressions?

To be honest, I'm surprised by how small it is. When I worked on the Continent I grew to love the huge fish markets. Even middling towns would have a good-sized fish market, and in cities like Barcelona and Paris they are many times the size of Billingsgate. For a people surrounded by a sea full of fresh fish, Brits are remarkably wary of eating them. You'll notice that a good many of the members of the public buying fish here are Chinese. That's a good sign; the Chinese love fish, but it has to be fresh – they also relish a bargain.

What's your favorite fish?

John Dory. And I'm not just saying that because there's a magnificent one just over there! The John Dory has the perfect combination of firm flesh and a delicate flavor, which means that you can do so much with it.

So how can you tell when you're getting really fresh fish?

Well, it's time to go on the offensive. Ask your fishmonger or the person behind the fish counter in the supermarket when they took delivery of their stock. Sometimes this may force them to lie to you, but however good or bad we are at judging the freshness of fish, we are all pretty good at spotting liars! Then take a serious look at the fish itself. Lift the gill covers and look at the gills (on the head, around about where their ears would be). If the gills are a deep pink or red, and if they look bright – not dull and slimy – that is a good sign. The tail should be well shaped and not ragged. The fish should be bright-eyed. If it's a flat fish the body should be firm – give it a prod with your finger – and it should feel "heavy;" if it feels light and flabby then it may be full of eggs, which means you're buying more roe than flesh. Most important of all, use your nose. Fresh fish doesn't smell, not even the guts. You'll notice that even a busy market like this one doesn't smell of fish.

There are some oysters over there. How do you open them at home?

Opening oysters is one of those skills which we would all be master of if only we got enough practice. At the restaurant we open about two thousand a week, so all the chefs are pretty good. Do not resort to those new-fangled oyster-opening gadgets – there's a thing like a pair of pliers which just crushes the edges of the shells until the oyster surrenders – you simply end up with gritty oysters. For most of us the best oyster-opening gadget is a fishmonger.

What are the main differences between Native Oysters and Rock Oysters?

Technically speaking, Natives are *Ostrea edulis* and Rocks are *Crassotrea gigas*. Rock oysters are also known as "Pacific" oysters and do well in warm water – which is why they do not follow the "only-when-there's-an-R-in-the-month" rule. The Native oyster is Britain's indigenous oyster, slower growing and a lover of cool water. There are less of them and they are more expensive. As to the taste, you have to be a regular and committed oyster eater to tell them apart in a blind tasting, but most people give the crown to Natives ... perhaps that's another reason why they are more expensive.

How do you tell a good oyster?

To start with they need to be firmly shut. When opened they should be wet, with surplus seawater sloshing around; they should be plump and glossy, and they should never smell nasty.

Which do you think is the most underrated fish?

I'd put two kinds of fish in joint first place – pollock and whiting. Admittedly they haven't got a very strong taste, but when fresh they are just the thing to use for fishcakes or fishsticks. They bind well and have the perfect texture for such dishes. They are also cheap.

I'm a big fan of crab. Which do you think is the better buy, a cock or a hen crab ?

I always pick a hen crab for myself, but that's because I prefer the brown meat, and although the claw – and thus the amount of white meat – is smaller on a hen crab, there's much more yummy brown meat.

How do you tell when a crab is fresh?

At the restaurant we always buy them alive. They should feel heavy and be energetic. If you are buying a crab that has already been cooked, you should look out for one where the brown meat is still shiny and has not gone dull. The "dead men's fingers" should be fluffy and not bedraggled.

While we are at it, what should you look out for when choosing a lobster?

There are two rules. The first is that you should choose one that is sweet-smelling and has a firm shell. The second is purely about size. If you have the option you should always choose a lobster that is between $2\frac{1}{2}$ and $4\frac{1}{2}$ pounds. Any larger than $4\frac{1}{2}$ pounds and the meat will be tough. Any smaller than $2\frac{1}{2}$ pounds and not only is the shell-to-meat ratio less favorable, but the meat tends to be watery. When you get a nice lobster weighing between $2\frac{1}{2}$ and $4\frac{1}{2}$ pounds, the claws will have grown big enough to contain plenty of meat, while the tail has not yet grown so large that it is tough.

I notice that the Livebait menu often stipulates "line caught" sea bass. How does this make a difference?

They are better fish. It's as simple as that. The ones that come from trawlers get rolled around in the nets and damaged; they also tend to bleed a lot, which spoils the fish. When fish are netted, the change of pressure as they are brought up to the surface can empty their stomachs, which leaves them flabby. You must also remember that trawlers stay out at sea for a lot longer than the smaller boats that fish with lines. Line-caught fish are usually fresher fish, so as well as being better for the environment, they make better eating.

I bet you'd tell me the same story about "diver caught" scallops?

Getting hold of large, fresh, top-quality scallops is even more of a headache. I like the ones we get from the divers in Scotland. The traditional scallop dredgers just tow a huge beam along the bottom of the sea, which scrapes up every living thing and leaves a featureless mud behind. It may take years for the seabed to regenerate. Divers can literally hand-pick the scallops, leaving the little ones to grow on. Of course, using divers can lead to unforeseen problems, especially in the winter when the weather is bad: one week, the divers working for our suppliers were trapped on a remote island in the West of Scotland by a fierce storm. For several days there was no sign of the divers and no sign of any scallops. We had to take them off the menu.

What's the difference between a brill and a turbot, and why do they call some fish chicken turbot?
I don't know why they are called "chicken," but the term is sometimes used for smaller
turbot – up to about 2 pounds. Chicken turbot are good eating, though not a patch on the
texture and flavor of a bigger fish. Turbot is slightly firmer, and has a more pronounced flavor
than brill. You can always tell a turbot because it is usually a lot darker than a brill and is
covered in warts, lumps, and spikes.

Two other fish that can often get confused are Dover and lemon soles. How do you tell them apart?
The Dover sole is a very classy fish, firm and full of flavor. The lemon sole is a definite second best – a poor person's sole. Once filleted, all manner of flat fish, right down to the humble dab, can be passed off by unscrupulous chefs as sole, but while some may look the same, and even taste similar, the texture is what shows them up immediately. Dover sole is so firm it is almost like meat.

Why do you insist on undyed smoked haddock in your recipes?

Don't be silly! When you taste something, are you likely to enjoy it more if it is a bright fluorescent yellow? Dye doesn't make the fish taste any different, and we certainly don't need to ingest any more chemicals than we already do.

You also seem to be a fan of wild salmon. Why's that?

Next time you have the opportunity, compare a wild salmon with his farmed brother. The wild fish will have a clean, streamlined look and a square tail; the farmed fish will have more of a couch potato look about him. This is not surprising – he has spent his lifetime in a cage. Also note the flabby, fatty flesh of the farmed salmon, and the tail and fins, which are often ragged. Wild salmon always eats better, but the salmon-farming industry is aware of these problems and is developing new ways to narrow the gap in quality. One of the most successful initiatives has been to relocate the salmon cages further out to sea in strong tidal currents, which is one way of guaranteeing the growing fish more exercise. So the rule is, wild salmon if you can get it and farmed salmon if you cannot, and the same rule applies when you're buying smoked salmon as well.

What's the most troublesome ingredient you use in the restaurant?

The one that gives us the most headaches is the langostino. Every day the demand for langostinos outstrips supply, and the UK market is put under even greater pressure by the Spanish, French, and Portuguese agents. Prices can soar with just a hint of bad weather. What's more, langostinos are very fragile; our suppliers deliver them alive, in seawater and each in its own rigid plastic tube to stop damage from fighting or accidents. You can tell when they are top quality: the langostinos are lively, and have good hard shells, especially around their heads. They are also the most wonderful eating; we put them on the menu steamed. No frills, just the natural sweetness of the fresh langostino . . . delicious.

What's the most rewarding thing about cooking fish?

At Livebait we get all sorts of customers, from the fish fanatics to people who rarely – if ever – choose fish when they are out. For so many Brits, eating fish begins and ends with battered cod and chips, so introducing them to the sweetness of a seared scallop or the wonderful texture of a piece of roasted brill is terribly exciting. Fish doesn't have to be full of bones; it doesn't have to be an oddity you eat only on Friday; it doesn't even have to be difficult to cook. Fish can be simple and delicious. When you see someone change their mind about fish, that's the most rewarding thing of all.

fish tales

Introduction

Most cookbooks are divided up into sections by ingredients, or by seasons of the year, or by particular courses of a meal. This one isn't. We thought it more helpful to divide the dishes into sections on the basis of who you would cook them for. This works well, if the restaurant is anything to judge by – a pair of young lovers enjoying a romantic date never order the same dishes as a businessman entertaining his bank manager, while at home you would cook different dishes for your family from the ones you could show off with at a grand dinner party.

So "Starters and suppers" contains all the recipes that would make good starters in a multi-course meal or informal supper dishes in their own right. "Family meals" means, well, meals for the family. "Grandstand dishes" are the ones for boasting about, which will enhance your reputation on the dinner-party circuit. "Dinners à deux" are recipes for two that err on the romantic and extravagant side. "Dishes from left field" take their name from the American expression "coming out of left field," which is a sporting term meaning completely unexpected and surprising. These are dishes that use novel combinations of ingredients or original techniques. They are generally pretty unusual and tend to be daring. "Breads," "Desserts," and "Pickles, preserves, and sauces" are all self-explanatory.

It only remains to proffer a touch of clarification.

- *Light olive oil* means standard, everyday, inexpensive olive oil.
- *Good olive oil* means extra virgin, the good stuff you keep for dressings and drizzling.
- *Eggs* are medium eggs – especially important in the baking recipes.
- *Salt* is sea salt.
- *Pepper* is freshly ground black pepper.
- Generally, the presentation suggested in the "Shopping and showing off" section for each dish, is tailored to the domestic kitchen. Sometimes, at the restaurant, dishes are arranged slightly differently. This is why some of the pictures (which were all taken at Livebait) show a more exotic and fanciful presentation. Rest assured, the dishes will taste just as good however they are plated up!

Weights and Measures

All recipes are written to imperial measures. They can be converted to metric using the following tables. Do not combine metric and imperial.

Liquid Conversions

Metric		Imperial
15 ml	=	$\frac{1}{2}$ fl oz
30 ml	=	1 fl oz
50 ml	=	2 fl oz
100 ml	=	$3\frac{1}{2}$ fl oz
125 ml	=	4 fl oz
150 ml	=	5 fl oz ($\frac{1}{4}$ pint)
200 ml	=	7 fl oz ($\frac{1}{3}$ pint)
250 ml ($\frac{1}{4}$ liter)	=	9 fl oz
300 ml	=	10 fl oz ($\frac{1}{2}$ pint)
350 ml	=	12 fl oz
400 ml	=	14 fl oz
425 ml	=	15 fl oz ($\frac{3}{4}$ pint)
450 ml	=	16 fl oz
500 ml ($\frac{1}{2}$ liter)	=	18 fl oz
600 ml	=	1 pint (20 fl oz)
700 ml	=	$1\frac{1}{4}$ pints
850 ml	=	$1\frac{1}{2}$ pints
1 liter	=	$1\frac{3}{4}$ pints
1.2 liters	=	2 pints
1.5 liters	=	$2\frac{3}{4}$ pints
2 liters	=	$3\frac{1}{2}$ pints
2.5 liters	=	$4\frac{1}{2}$ pints
3 liters	=	$5\frac{1}{4}$ pints

Solid Weight Conversions

Metric		Imperial
15 g	=	$\frac{1}{2}$ oz
25 g	=	1 oz
40 g	=	$1\frac{1}{2}$ oz
50 g	=	$1\frac{3}{4}$ oz
75 g	=	$2\frac{3}{4}$ oz
100 g	=	$3\frac{1}{2}$ oz
125 g	=	$4\frac{1}{2}$ oz
150 g	=	$5\frac{1}{2}$ oz
175 g	=	6 oz
200 g	=	7 oz
225 g	=	8 oz
250 g	=	9 oz
275 g	=	$9\frac{1}{2}$ oz
300 g	=	$10\frac{1}{2}$ oz
325 g	=	$11\frac{1}{2}$ oz
350 g	=	12 oz
400 g	=	14 oz
425 g	=	15 oz
450 g	=	1 lb
500 g	=	1 lb 2 oz
600 g	=	1 lb 5 oz
700 g	=	1 lb 9 oz
750 g	=	1 lb 10 oz
1 kg	=	2 lb 4 oz
1.25 kg	=	2 lb 12 oz
1.5 kg	=	3 lb 5 oz
2 kg	=	4 lb 8 oz
2.25 kg	=	5 lb
2.5 kg	=	5 lb 8 oz
3 kg	=	6 lb 8 oz

Oven Temperature Conversions

°C	Gas	°F
110	$\frac{1}{4}$	225
120	$\frac{1}{2}$	250
140	1	275
150	2	300
160	3	325
175	4	350
190	5	375
200	6	400
220	7	425
230	8	450
240	9	475
260	10	500

Standards Liquid

1 teaspoon	=	5 ml
1 dessertspoon	=	10 ml
1 tablespoon	=	15 ml

starters and suppers

Gigandaes plaki

You do need to remember to put the beans in to soak a day or so earlier, but from then on this recipe has few pitfalls. The result is stunning. If you can find the large Greek bean called gigandaes, use them; otherwise the dish works as well with the humble lima bean. Serves four of the hungriest.

2$\frac{1}{2}$ cups dried gigandaes

2$\frac{1}{4}$ cups Chicken Stock (see page 188)

2 teaspoons salt

2 cups diced celery (about $\frac{1}{2}$ head)

1$\frac{1}{4}$ cups diced carrots

1$\frac{1}{4}$ cups finely chopped shallots

1$\frac{1}{4}$ cups finely chopped leeks

4 cloves garlic

14$\frac{1}{2}$ ounce can whole tomatoes

3 bay leaves

$\frac{1}{3}$ cup good olive oil

1 Soak the beans for 24 hours, refrigerated.

2 Cover with cold water and bring up to a boil. Simmer for an hour, or until the beans are just soft, stirring occasionally to prevent sticking.

3 Then add the chicken stock and salt.

4 Dice the celery and carrots, finely chop the shallots and leeks, peel and crush the garlic, strain the tomatoes from their juice. Add them all, plus the bay leaves, to the pan with the beans, cover and cook together for 30 minutes.

5 Ten minutes before serving, take the pot off the stove and adjust the seasoning, remove the bay leaves, then stir in the olive oil. Replace the lid.

Shopping and showing off

You may substitute mild onions for shallots. You can use plain water if you have no chicken stock on hand. If you are using dried lima beans, mix large and small types.

Home-cured mackerel

and scrambled eggs

This recipe makes a delicious hot supper dish – just pile the eggs and mackerel onto toast – but also becomes an elegant starter when presented cold, turned out of ramekins onto a plate with a green salad. Serves four.

4 zucchini

a little good olive oil

$\frac{1}{4}$ pound (1 stick) butter

8 eggs

pepper

$\frac{1}{4}$ cup heavy cream

4 fillets Home-cured Mackerel (see page 202)

1 Cut the zucchini into thin strips lengthwise. Brush with oil and place under a hot broiler for a minute until wilted. Use them to line 4 ramekins – they should be big enough to hold $\frac{3}{4}$ cup.

2 Melt the butter in a thick-bottomed pan. Stir the eggs together with four twists of ground black pepper, and add to the butter.

3 Stir over low heat until the eggs start to set. Just before you are left with a solid rubbery mass, take the pan away from the heat and work in the cream. Allow to cool.

4 Skin and flake the mackerel and stir it into the egg mixture. Beware; if you add the mackerel while the mixture is too hot it will "cook," which accentuates the fishy taste.

5 Pack this mixture into the ramekins and cool before turning out.

Shopping and showing off

This rich dish benefits from some contrasting flavors on the plate – try a salad made from arugula or radicchio leaves and a little Balsamic Vinaigrette (see page 193).

Brandade mashed potatoes
with poached eggs and pak choi

This dish will bring out the forward planner in you. It's very tasty, but you must start at least a day ahead. At Livebait, Brandade Mashed Potatoes do sterling service as a vegetable, but with a poached egg and some greens they make a great supper. This recipe makes enough for four.

9 ounces salt cod

$2\frac{1}{4}$ cups skim milk

I bay leaf

2 cloves garlic

I large fat red chili pepper

$\frac{1}{4}$ cup olive oil

$1\frac{1}{4}$ pounds floury potatoes

juice of I lemon

pepper

4 fresh eggs

a bunch of pak choi

I Rehydrate the cod by putting it in fresh water to soak for 8 hours; then change the water and leave it for another 8 hours; then repeat the procedure a third time, by which time your piece of cod will be considerably bigger.

2 Infuse the milk with the bay leaf by bringing to a boil and leaving to simmer for 20 minutes.

3 Peel and crush the garlic; seed and chop the chili peppers finely; cook in a frying pan with a little of the oil until they are softened.

4 Add the salt cod to the milk and cook until it flakes easily – about 35–40 minutes. Strain off the milk and reserve.

5 Pick off the skin, remove any bones, and then flake the fish into a bowl.

6 Peel and boil the potatoes without salt. You want them fairly firm – definitely not mushy. Drain and mash.

7 Beat half the warm milk, the olive oil and the lemon juice into the mashed potatoes.

8 Add the sautéed chili and garlic, and finally the cod. Mix thoroughly and adjust seasoning. You'll need pepper but probably no more salt.

9 Poach the eggs and wilt the pak choi in boiling water.

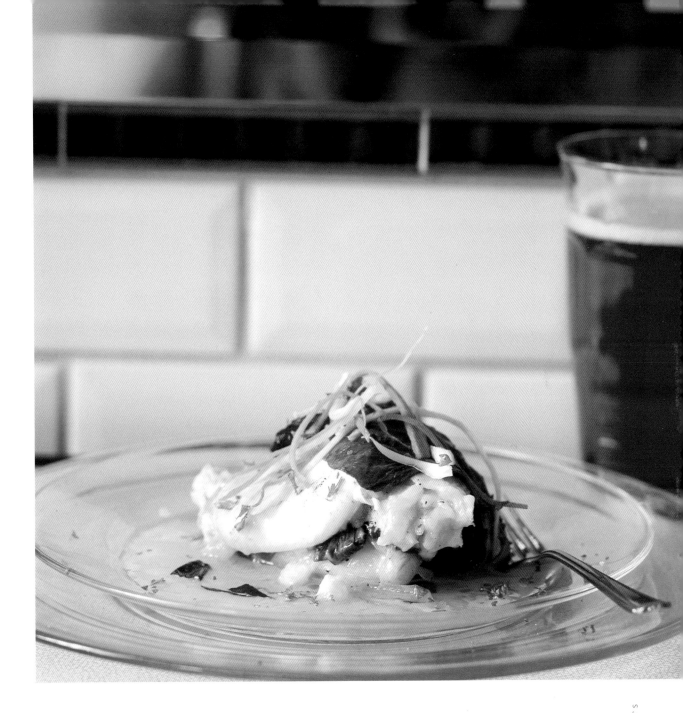

Shopping and showing off

You'll find salt cod in some supermarkets and delicatessens. Pak choi is a crisp Chinese vegetable that is increasingly common in supermarkets and always to be found in Chinese shops; spinach is a fine substitute. You can cook the Brandade Mashed Potatoes in advance, but they are difficult to reheat without burning – unless you resort to a microwave.

Salade "niçoise"

Those pedantic people who argue about the correct ingredients of a classic salade niçoise would doubtless be very upset by the Livebait version. No tuna or anchovies, but prosciutto and cooking sake ...! Try eating it. Whatever it is called makes little difference – it eats very well indeed. Salad for four.

4 ounces fine green beans

1 artichoke

$\frac{1}{2}$ red pepper

$\frac{1}{2}$ green pepper

2 ounces prosciutto

4 plum tomatoes

1 ripe pear

$\frac{1}{3}$ cup finely chopped shallots

4 small heads Belgian endive

12 black olives, pitted

3 tablespoons snipped chives

1 tablespoon freshly squeezed lemon juice

$\frac{1}{2}$ cup good olive oil plus a little extra

$\frac{1}{4}$ cup mirin (sweet cooking sake)

salt

1 Blanch the beans in boiling salted water for 3 minutes, remove, and plunge into icy cold water to maintain the color.

2 Boil the artichoke until it is cooked. Remove the two outer layers of leaves to reveal the central choke of hairy fibers. Cut the choke out with a teaspoon. Slice the heart into strips.

3 Chop the peppers into thin strips.

4 Cut the prosciutto into thin strips and fry until crisp in a minimum amount of olive oil. Dry and cool on kitchen paper.

5 Peel and seed the plum tomatoes, and cut them into strips.

6 Peel and core the pear. Cut into slices lengthways.

7 Peel the shallots and chop them finely.

8 Rinse and trim the endives. Peel off the leaves keeping them whole.

9 Combine the beans, artichoke, peppers, ham, tomatoes, pear, shallots, endives, olives and chives in a salad bowl.

10 Make the dressing in a bowl by whisking together the lemon juice, oil and mirin. Add salt to taste.

11 Toss the salad gently with the dressing and serve.

Shopping and showing off

Pears: if you can find them, large Asian pears are particularly good, otherwise a large Anjou pear is fine. Mirin is a sweet sake specially made for cooking. You'll find it in most supermarkets. You need the kind of Belgian endive called witloof. Radicchio is *not* suitable. Room temperature: both the tomatoes and the pear will taste better if served at room temperature.

Shrimp and mussel sauerkraut

At Livebait, this unlikely-sounding concoction is served as a side dish. But when you taste it you will discover that it is good enough to stand alone. Seriously delicious, and very simple. Serves four.

1 cup sauerkraut

4 tablespoons unsalted butter

10 ounces mussels – meat only

$\frac{2}{3}$ cup dry white wine

8 peeled, cooked jumbo shrimp

a bunch of dill

1 Rinse the sauerkraut in a colander under the tap. Cut the butter into cubes and put it into the refrigerator to chill.

2 If you are using fresh mussels, open them by shaking them in a pan over a low flame. Pick them over, discarding any that have not opened. Shell the rest and reserve the meat.

4 Heat the sauerkraut through in a nonreactive pan with the wine.

5 When it is hot add the shrimp and mussels and allow them to heat through.

6 Strain off the liquid into another pan to finish the sauce. Put the lid back on and keep the sauerkraut warm.

7 Bring the juices to a boil. Take the cold butter and whisk it into a boiling sauce so that it thickens and becomes glossy.

8 Take the pan off the heat and stir the sauce back into the sauerkraut. Snip the dill into the mixture and stir in. Heat through and serve immediately.

Shopping and showing off

Sauerkraut comes in large jars or cans and is available in most supermarkets. Experiment to find which brand is least salty. Shrimp that are "shell on" are often a better value as you are not paying high prices for the water glaze covering that you get on frozen ones. It is important not to overcook the mussels and shrimps, as they will become rubbery if you do. This dish makes an original accompaniment to all kinds of plainly cooked fish.

Chickpea, red wine and black pudding stew

You shouldn't let the requirement for forward planning put you off trying this heartwarming stew, which is loosely based on the Iberian dish cocido. Start 24 hours in advance. Serves four hungry people.

2$\frac{1}{2}$ cups dried chickpeas

4$\frac{1}{4}$ cups chicken stock

1$\frac{1}{4}$ cups diced carrots

2 cups peeled shallots

3 stalks celery

4 cloves garlic

1 bay leaf

1$\frac{1}{2}$ cups red wine – not your best!

1 pound black pudding

salt and pepper

2 tablespoons light olive oil

1 Soak the chickpeas in water for 24 hours, refrigerated.

2 Strain the chickpeas, rinse them in fresh water and put them in a pot with the chicken stock. Bring to a boil, turn down the heat, cover the pan and simmer for 45 minutes.

3 Dice the vegetables, peel and slice the garlic, and add to the pot with the wine and bay leaf. Simmer for 30 minutes more.

4 Take 4 ounces of the black pudding, skin it, chop it up, and stir into the stew to thicken the juices; adjust the seasoning to taste.

5 Cut the remaining black pudding into slices on the bias (i.e., diagonally, across) and cook quickly in a hot frying pan with a little oil to crisp up the outside.

6 Ladle the stew into a soup bowl and top with some of the fried black pudding.

Shopping and showing off

How to choose a black pudding (blood sausage) is a very personal matter: they range all the way from highly perfumed, large-diameter, commercially made puddings, to smaller, harder ring sausages handmade by butchers. Small-diameter puddings seem to fry crisper.

Lime polenta fries with mayonnaise

A dish to upset every living Belgian! Crisp on the outside and soft inside, these fries work well with any mayonnaise from the luxurious and homemade to the bottled and shop bought.

2 fleshy red chili peppers

10 scallions

1 bunch cilantro

3 cups water

salt and pepper

$1\frac{1}{2}$ cups instant polenta

zest and juice of 4 limes

$\frac{1}{3}$ cup olive oil

oil for deep frying

mayonnaise

1 Seed and chop the chilies very finely. Chop the scallions and the cilantro. Put them to one side.

2 Bring the water to a boil and add 1 tablespoon of salt.

3 Add the polenta and stir continually while it thickens into a porridge.

4 Lower the heat and add the lime zest and juice, the chilis, the scallions, the cilantro, and the olive oil. Keep stirring until well mixed. Adjust the seasoning with salt and pepper – it may need salt.

5 Pour into a large tray (so that the polenta is no deeper than ¾ inch) and place in the refrigerator.

6 When completely cold and set, cut into large pieces (3 × ¾ × ¾-inch).

7 Roll the pieces in flour and deep-fry in hot oil (preferably olive oil) for 4–5 minutes, until crisp and cooked.

Shopping and showing off

This is a simple dish that you can vary to suit your taste: experiment with different flavorings. Store-bought mayonnaise is fine; simple is best.

starters and suppers

Salmon and dill ravioli

If you can get fresh ravioli pasta from a helpful Italian delicatessen, do so – but you will miss out on the fun of making your own. Makes sixteen generous ravioli.

¾ pound raw salmon

½ cup crème fraîche *or* sour cream

1 bunch fresh dill

salt and pepper

1 teaspoon fresh paprika

1 quantity Simple Pasta Dough (see page 200)

1 Skin and bone the salmon, chop it into small dice, and put it in a bowl. Add the crème fraîche. Snip the dill and stir it all together. Season well with salt, pepper and the paprika.

2 Roll out the dough as thin as possible. Then cut out pairs of circles about 4 inches across. Put a good dollop of the mixture in the center of each one and superimpose the lid. Use your fingers to crimp the edges shut. Be firm!

3 Poach in salty boiling water to which a tiny bit of olive oil has been added. The ravioli will only take 7–8 minutes, or maybe a little longer depending on the thickness of the pasta. Do no more than three at a time unless you have a very big pan. Keep warm until you serve.

Shopping and showing off

For a starter serve three of these ravioli with a dribble of melted butter and some green leaves. As a supper dish, try four with a dipping sauce – a puddle of the simple Pernod Sauce goes well (see page 194).

Smoked haddock and cockle quiche

You can substitute octopus for cockles in this simple but delicious dish. Then it becomes the perfect way to use up any spare partly cooked octopus you may have left over after making recipes like the one on page 114 for Honey and Ginger Roast Octopus. Serves four as a generous starter.

1 frozen single-shell pie pastry

2 tablespoons butter

$\frac{1}{2}$ cup chopped leeks

$\frac{1}{2}$ cup chopped shallots

$\frac{1}{2}$ cup chopped carrots

1 tablespoon light olive oil

4 ounces smoked haddock

4 ounces shelled cockles

3 eggs

$\frac{1}{3}$ cup crème fraîche

$\frac{1}{3}$ cup heavy cream

$\frac{1}{2}$ bunch tarragon

1 ounce capers

salt and pepper to taste

1 Preheat your oven to 450°F.

2 Butter a deep tart pan – 8 inches in diameter by at least 1 inch deep.

3 Fit the pastry to the dish. Prick the base with a fork. Butter a piece of foil and line the inside of the pastry case, fitting it closely to the sides. Fill with dried beans and bake for 7–8 minutes, until the pastry is set but only just.

4 Remove the liner and prick the base again. Press the sides up if they have started to slip down. Replace the liner and beans and cook for another 5 minutes. Now the pastry should be cooked but not colored.

5 Remove the liner and bake for a further 2–3 minutes until the pastry is nicely colored. Let the oven cool down to 375°F.

6 Allow the pastry to cool in the dish and then take it out . . . very carefully.

7 Meanwhile, peel and chop the leeks, shallots and carrots and cook in olive oil until softened.

8 Skin the haddock and cut it into chunks. Rinse the cockles.

9 Beat together the eggs, crème fraîche, and heavy cream. Strip the tarragon leaves from the stalks, chop them coarsely and add them. Add the capers. Season the mixture – be careful with the salt but it may need some.

10 Put a sheet of baking parchment on to a baking sheet and put the tart pan on it. Put the mixed fish and vegetables in, and then add the egg mixture so that it is filled to within $\frac{1}{4}$ inch of the rim. Bake for 30 minutes.

Shopping and showing off

Following this method you can make the quiche base a day ahead and fill and cook it only when required. If you can find fresh cockles, so much the better – if not, frozen or pickled ones will suffice. This quiche begs to be served with a small salad – a few mixed leaves, preferably undressed; otherwise the dressing would fight with the flavors of the quiche. You can serve the quiche hot or cold, but if cold, try and make it more like "room temperature" or lukewarm; the flavors will be much improved.

Potato and hazelnut gratin

This makes a splendid supper dish with the addition of a few slices of well-crisped bacon to give a contrasting texture. It also makes a great support act: try it with the Baked Whole Porgy (see page 92). Serves four.

$\frac{3}{4}$ cup hazelnuts, unblanched

$\frac{3}{4}$ cup heavy cream

salt, pepper and nutmeg

$2\frac{1}{4}$ pounds potatoes

2 tablespoons warm butter

2 cloves garlic

1 Preheat your oven to 425°F.

2 Prepare the hazelnuts by roasting them for 4–5 minutes on a tray in the hot oven. Remove – turn the oven down to 300°F – and as the nuts cool, rub off the skins with your fingers. Crush them with a pestle and mortar, or by folding them in a dish towel and rolling a bottle over them. Your objective is small chunky pieces, not dust.

3 Bring the cream to a boil, season with salt and pepper and some grated nutmeg.

4 Peel and then slice the potatoes paper thin, using a mandoline if you have one. Rinse in cold water to get rid of excess starch, then add them to the cream.

5 Use half the butter to grease a large gratin dish – pick one big enough (it is important that your finished layer of potato mixture is no more than $\frac{3}{4}$ inch thick) or prepare four ramekins. Crush the garlic and spread over the bottom of the dish or dishes.

6 Lift out the potato slices with a slotted spoon and arrange two or three layers of them in the dish; then dribble on a layer of cream; then a layer of hazelnuts; then cream; then potatoes; then cream; then potatoes; then hazelnuts.

7 Cover with foil and bake for 60 minutes for a large gratin dish and 30 minutes for ramekins. Check whether the potato is cooked by testing with a knife through the foil. Then remove the foil and allow to brown. If necessary brown the top still further under a broiler before serving.

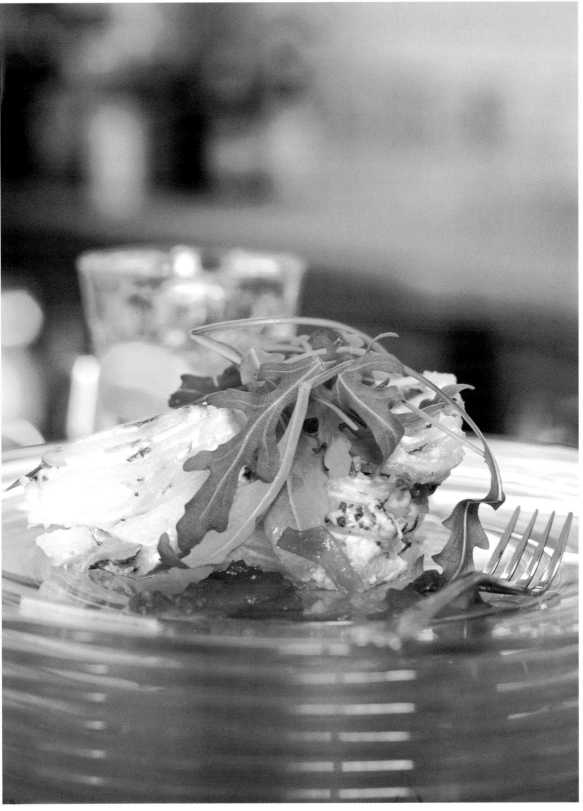

Egg tagliatelle

with mussels and Merguez sausage

Merguez is a fatty, seriously spicy lamb sausage. If you cannot find it, feel free to substitute another spicy sausage – just remember spiciness is key. This dish started life playing a supporting role in the Tiger Shrimp and Sea Bass dish on page 94, but it soon became obvious that it had claims to be a dish in its own right. Serves four as a generous starter, or three as a supper.

2$\frac{1}{4}$ pounds mussels

1 red onion

1 clove of garlic

1 fat red chili pepper

$\frac{1}{4}$ cup olive oil

7 ounces Merguez or other spicy sausage

18 ounces fresh *or* dried egg tagliatelle

salt

2 eggs

$\frac{2}{3}$ cup heavy cream

$\frac{1}{2}$ bunch fresh parsley

pepper

1 Steam the mussels until they open and pick out the meat; discard any that remain closed.

2 Finely chop the onion, crush the garlic, seed and chop the chili – then cook them in a large frying pan with a little of the olive oil until they soften.

3 While this is happening, prick the sausages with a fork to stop them bursting and blanch them for 3–4 minutes in a large pan of boiling water. Take out with a slotted spoon and cut into 2-inch slices.

4 Bring the cooking water back to a boil and add 2 teaspoons of salt, 1 tablespoon of olive oil and the tagliatelle. Cook for 2–3 minutes; the pasta should be perceptibly undercooked. Strain off the water.

5 Beat together the egg and cream in a bowl with the snipped parsley leaves. Set aside.

6 Add the sausage slices to the onion mixture in the frying pan and make sure they are cooked through. Add the mussels and the remaining olive oil. Stir the mixture. Add the pasta and pour over the egg and cream mixture; mix thoroughly over low heat until everything is warmed through. Adjust seasoning and serve immediately.

French beans tarator

At Livebait this is one of the more straightforward vegetable accompaniments on offer – crunchy French beans with a rich walnut sauce. It makes a splendid starter, and if you feel adventurous and spendthrift you could always substitute Brazil nuts for the walnuts – it will at least save you the chore of shelling the walnuts. Serves four as a starter or six in its role as an accompanying vegetable.

4 slices of your favorite white bread

$\frac{2}{3}$ cup good olive oil

2 cups shelled walnuts *or* Brazil nuts

2 cloves garlic, peeled

$\frac{1}{2}$ cup balsamic vinegar

salt, pepper and sweet paprika to taste

1 pound extra fine French beans

1 Cut the crusts from the bread and soften the bread in a little water, then squeeze it dry by hand. Put it in a food processor or blender and, with the motor on slow, gradually add the oil, then the nuts (if you're using Brazils it is sensible to prechop them a bit with a heavy knife), peeled garlic cloves and the vinegar. When you have a sauce with a smooth, creamy consistency adjust the seasoning – salt, pepper and sweet paprika.

2 Top and tail the beans, and then blanch them in boiling salted water for 3–4 minutes.

3 Put the sauce and the beans into a dry pan and warm through. Do not let it get too hot or the sauce will separate.

Shopping and showing off

At Livebait we make the Tarator Sauce using Sun-dried Tomato Bread (see page 153) but any good, firm bread will do. The more character the bread has the better, but very dense wholemeal breads do not absorb as much oil, and you may have to drizzle some extra on to the plate to lubricate the dish.

Goat's cheese cheesecake

This makes a good starter (experiment with individual parcels) or a great family supper dish as a single large cheesecake. Serves four.

2 sheets from a packet of phyllo pastry

4 tablespoons butter, melted

3 tablespoons Red Onion Jam (see page 182)

1 cup grated Parmesan

4 ounces curd goat's cheese *or* any soft, mild goat's cheese

$^1/_3$ cup crème fraîche

2 eggs

1 teaspoon paprika

salt and pepper

1 quantity Tomato Chutney (see page 180)

1 Preheat your oven to 325°F.

2 Line an 8-inch loose-bottomed tart pan with 2 layers of phyllo pastry, brushing the first with butter before adding the second. Leave as much phyllo as possible overhanging the edge.

3 Use a food processor or blender to combine the onion jam, Parmesan, goat's cheese, crème fraîche and eggs. Season with the paprika, and salt and pepper to taste.

4 Pour the mixture into the center of the phyllo and fold in the edges. Brush the top with melted butter.

5 Bake for 2–3 hours. Start testing after two hours. The cake is done when a knife driven into the center and withdrawn feels hot on the lips.

Shopping and showing off

Curd goat's cheese will give you the best possible combination of taste and texture: ask for it at a cheese shop or the supermarket cheese counter. You can serve this cheesecake with a good dollop of Tomato Chutney.

starters and suppers

42

Smoked haddock,
leek and potato broth with quail's eggs

This is a rich broth containing good-sized chunks of haddock and finished with quail's eggs that are allowed to poach in each bowl of boiling soup on the way to the table. The recipe will serve four as a starter or make a good supper for two.

2¼ pounds plum tomatoes

salt and pepper

1 bunch basil

½ bunch parsley

½ bunch thyme

½ pound leeks

½ pound waxy potatoes (like Yellow Finn)

1 pound smoked haddock fillet

4¼ cups Chicken Stock (see page 188) or Vegetable Stock (see page 189)

½ teaspoon smoked hot paprika

4 quail's eggs

1 Preheat your oven to 250°F – it shouldn't take long!

2 Cut the tomatoes in half lengthwise and arrange them on a baking sheet, sprinkle with sea salt and pepper, and half of the basil, parsley and thyme. Bake in the oven for 2 hours until they are wrinkled and dry-looking. Allow to cool, and purée them in a food processor.

3 Wash the leeks and cut into ¾-inch lengths. Peel and dice the potatoes.

4 Skin the haddock fillets and chop them into large bite-sized pieces.

5 Bring the stock to a boil in a large pot. Add the tomato purée and stir until amalgamated. Reduce the heat and simmer for 10 minutes.

6 Add the leeks and potatoes and simmer for a further 25 minutes until the potatoes are cooked but still firm.

7 Add the remaining herbs, the smoked paprika, and the pieces of haddock; simmer for a further 5 minutes. Adjust the seasoning with salt and pepper.

Shopping and showing off

If you cannot find smoked paprika, ordinary paprika will do – although it is not as tasty. If you use the vegetable stock option this becomes a good dish for non meat-eaters. To serve, pour a boiling broth into the bowls, making sure that the bits of fish are evenly distributed, and crack a quail's egg into the center of the soup. The heat will poach the tiny egg on the way to the table.

family
meals

Halibut parcels in romaine lettuce with avgolemono sauce and baby vegetables (*see opposite*) 48   Smoked haddock, potato and parsnip rösti, sautéed spinach and poached eggs 50   **Panfried turmeric mullet with Middle Eastern rice and cumin sauce 52**   Steamed fillet of sole with lentils 54   **Deviled herrings with roast beets and turmeric potatoes 56**   Hotpot of cod cheeks, globe artichokes and button mushrooms with potato bread and aïoli 58   **Broiled red mullet with gigandaes plaki and tapenade 61**   Roast cod with couscous crust served with chickpea, red wine and black pudding stew 62   **Broiled polenta cake, roast tomatoes and tsatsiki 64**   John Dory, spinach and potato pie with Pernod sauce 66   **Tuna with honey-roast chicken wings and lentil stew 69**   Seared sea scallops with red wine pears 70   **Fisherman's soup 75**   Seared salmon with potato, cilantro and lemongrass dauphinoise, and an artichoke dressing 77   **Broiled smoked sturgeon with "nero" spinach and paprika sour cream 78**   Roast monkfish tail with braised red cabbage 80

Halibut parcels in romaine lettuce
with avgolemono sauce and baby vegetables

The sauce that smothers these halibut parcels and baby vegetables is derived from the famous Greek soup made from eggs and lemons – a combination of ingredients that at first glance seem to have "curdle" written all over them. Follow the simple steps and you'll end up with an interesting frothy sauce that is both rich and tangy – perfect with the sweet fish and young vegetables. Serves four.

16 outside leaves from 2 large romaine lettuces

$^3/_4$ pound raw shrimp

8 thin *or* 4 fat scallions

1 tablespoon sweet paprika

8 chunks halibut, weighing about 2 ounces each

12 baby carrots

12 baby fennel bulbs

12 baby leeks

12 shallots

2 cups Chicken Stock (see page 188)

$^2/_3$ cup white wine

1 tablespoon cornflour

3 eggs, separated

juice of 2 small lemons *or* 1 large

salt and pepper

1 Wilt the lettuce leaves in boiling water and refresh them in cold water; this will make them manageable.

2 Shell the shrimp, and remove the black veins that run down their backs; mince or chop them very finely. Chop the scallions finely. Mix with the shrimp.

3 Spread the mixture onto the lettuce leaves, place a bit of halibut on top of each, dust with paprika, then more shrimp, then roll up into neat parcels. If necessary, use two leaves per parcel to make a watertight envelope. Put to one side.

4 Peel and trim as necessary and then put the whole baby carrots, fennel, leeks and shallots into the bottom of a large pot and add the chicken stock and wine. Bring to a boil, then simmer for 20 minutes.

5 Carefully place the fish parcels on top of the vegetables and cook with the lid on for another 8–10 minutes, no more, depending on the thickness of your parcels.

6 Gently tip all the liquid from the pot into another pan to finish the sauce, holding back the vegetables and fish with the lid.

7 Mix the cornflour in a little cold water and whisk into the liquid.

8 Simmer until thickened, then turn off the heat.

9 Whisk the egg whites in a bowl until they peak, then fold in the yolks.

10 Pour the warm stock into the egg mixture, stirring with a whisk. Put the bowl over a saucepan of boiling water and gradually whisk in the lemon juice. Continue to whisk until the sauce thickens like custard. Adjust seasoning with salt and pepper.

11 Return the sauce to the pot of fish parcels and vegetables; leave for 5 minutes to amalgamate the flavors before serving.

Shopping and showing off

Either steaks of a large halibut or fillets from a small halibut work well with this dish. Baby vegetables are widely available in supermarkets, but if you cannot find any, substitute uniformly sized batons cut from ordinary vegetables. Serve in a soup bowl.

Smoked haddock, potato and parsnip rösti, sautéed spinach and poached eggs

The strength of this dish lies in the array of textures it provides. There's the fish, the crisp rösti, the spinach ... and just when you think it's all sounding a bit too dry there's the poached egg yolk. Delightful. Serves six.

1 $\frac{1}{4}$ pounds large potatoes

1 $\frac{1}{4}$ pounds parsnips

2 bunches scallions

1 bunch chervil

salt and black pepper

$\frac{1}{2}$ cup good olive oil

6 4-ounce smoked haddock fillets

1 garlic clove

4 tablespoons butter

1 $\frac{1}{4}$ pounds washed spinach

4 eggs

2 $\frac{1}{4}$ cups water

$\frac{1}{2}$ cup white wine vinegar

1 Preheat your oven and a flat baking sheet to 425°F.

2 Peel the potatoes and parsnips and grate them into a large bowl. Chop the scallions and the chervil and add them. Season with salt and pepper. Mix thoroughly, adding $\frac{1}{4}$ cup of the olive oil.

3 Cook the rösti in two batches. Heat a large frying pan with 2 tablespoons of the oil in it. Press half the rösti mixture into the hot pan in a flat layer.

4 Cook over moderately high heat until the bottom crisps up. Then turn it over onto the hot baking sheet. Repeat with the second batch of mixture.

5 Oil the haddock fillets and put them onto another baking sheet.

6 Put both the sheets into the oven for 10 minutes (the rösti should get the hottest part of your oven – probably the top). Check the rösti after 5 minutes.

7 In the meantime, crush the garlic. Put the remaining 1 tablespoon of oil in a large pan, and cook the garlic until it begins to soften. Add the spinach and stir until it has wilted completely. Press out the liquid that has formed while cooking, season and keep warm.

8 Poach the eggs in the water and vinegar. You are aiming for a runny yolk. Skin the haddock.

Shopping and showing off

To serve, cut a wedge from the rösti – or punch out a small circular rösti using a pastry-cutter – and crown it with the spinach, haddock and, finally, the poached egg. Part of the fun of this "tall food" is the joy of being a vandal as you push it over with your knife and fork.

Panfried turmeric mullet

with Middle Eastern rice and cumin sauce

Striped mullet is a meaty and much underrated fish. Make sure your fishmonger fillets it carefully for you – and the bigger the fish the better. If possible, always choose mullet caught on the open sea (at Livebait, we get some splendid ones from Guernsey). Estuarine fish can taste "muddy." The accompanying rice dish is straight from the spice markets and is deliciously squelchy. Accompany it with Cumin Sauce (page 197).

1 teaspoon cumin seeds

1 teaspoon coriander seeds

1 $\frac{1}{2}$ cups finely chopped Spanish onions

1 $\frac{1}{2}$ cups finely chopped leeks

a little olive oil

2 $\frac{1}{4}$ pounds leaf spinach

1 bunch basil

$\frac{1}{2}$ cup long grain rice

1 teaspoon ground cinnamon

2 tablespoons ground turmeric

$\frac{1}{2}$ cup raisins

juice of 1 lemon

4 tablespoons good olive oil

salt and pepper

2 ounces flour

1 tablespoon salt

4 striped mullet fillets each weighing about 6 ounces

3 tablespoons olive oil

1 quantity Cumin Sauce (see page 197)

1 In a dry frying pan toast the cumin and coriander seeds; crush them, using a pestle and mortar, or a grinder.

2 Cook the onions and leeks in a large saucepan over low heat with a little oil until they have softened. Add the cumin and coriander.

3 Wash the spinach, remove the stalks, and tear it up roughly by hand. Tear up the basil. Add them both to the saucepan, then turn down the heat as low as possible, and put the lid on for a minute or two until the spinach is soft.

4 Add the rice with ¾ cup of water, the cinnamon and a tablespoon of turmeric. Put the lid back on and cook slowly for 30 minutes, stirring occasionally and adding more water if the contents get dry.

5 The rice should be quite sloppy. When it's cooked add the raisins and the lemon juice and stir well. Then stir in 4 tablespoons good olive oil and leave to stand off the heat with the lid on. Adjust seasoning.

6 Mix the flour with a tablespoon of turmeric and salt and use it to coat the mullet fillets.

7 Fry the fillets in a little hot olive oil. They will be done after about 3 minutes a side.

Shopping and showing off

Mullet is one of those fish that needs to be very fresh. If you cannot find striped mullet with a sparkle in their eyes, change the plan and use a nice Dover sole. To serve, make an island of rice in the center of the plate – use a pastry ring or mold to make the rice "island" perfectly regular – then top with a fillet of fish, and surround with the Cumin Sauce.

Steamed fillet of sole with lentils

As Theodore's mother would say, "This is a Sunday dish." It's rich and earthy, with a combination of flavors that works well together – a genuinely unfussy dish that may not look elegant on the plate but that certainly stars in the taste department. Serves four.

I quantity Lentil Stew (see page 201)

9 ounces bulb fennel

I orange

$\frac{1}{3}$ cup crème fraîche

4 sole fillets

salt and pepper

a little butter

balsamic vinegar

good olive oil

1 Prepare the lentil stew in advance using the recipe on page 201. It will keep for up to a day.
2 Chop the fennel very finely; peel, seed and take all the pith off the orange segments before chopping them roughly. Mix them, and the fennel, into the crème fraîche.
3 Season each sole fillet with salt and pepper, and then roll it up like a jam roll using a quarter of the crème fraîche mixture as the "jam."
4 Wrap each fillet in buttered foil and stab a few holes in the parcel. Steam until cooked – about 10–15 minutes. The parcel will be firm when pressed.

Shopping and showing off

Get your fishmonger to fillet a large sole – Dover for preference, but you can substitute any true sole. Do not settle for one of the many flounders that are often sold as "sole" in the U.S. Try to get a large fish – around $1\frac{1}{2}$ pounds – that way a single fillet makes a fine portion. If you cannot find such a fish you may have to buy two and double up. To present the dish, unwrap the sole – any buttery juices can be added to the lentils – and arrange a mound of lentils on each plate. Then drizzle over some balsamic vinegar (cider vinegar would make an acceptable substitute) and a little good olive oil. If you are using a large fish, cut each fillet in half to give two "roulade" slices. Arrange these on the lentils on each plate.

Deviled herrings

with roast beets and turmeric potatoes

The herring is a rich and oily fish, well able to look after itself in the company of these powerful flavors. The tradition of "deviling" fish and meats is an old and honorable one, although the Livebait style owes more to North African influences than is usual. Serves four.

3 teaspoons cumin seeds

2 teaspoons cayenne pepper

2 teaspoons sea salt

$\frac{1}{3}$ cup light olive oil

2 eggs

8 large herring fillets

3 raw beets

I tablespoon honey

2 bay leaves

I $\frac{1}{4}$ pounds new potatoes

I teaspoon turmeric

I fat red chili pepper

2 garlic cloves

$\frac{1}{2}$ bunch fresh cilantro

I $\frac{1}{2}$ cups crisp breadcrumbs

$\frac{1}{4}$ cup yogurt

1 Preheat your oven to 400°F.

2 Prepare the deviling mix for the herrings. Take a pestle and mortar and grind up the cumin seeds with the cayenne and a teaspoon of the salt. Make into a paste with 2 teaspoons of the olive oil. Beat this mixture into the eggs.

3 Marinate the herring fillets in the spicy egg wash while you prepare the vegetables.

4 Put the beets into a roasting tray with ¾ cup of water, the honey and the bay leaves. Roast for about 60 minutes.

5 Wash, but do not peel, the new potatoes. Then dice them. Put 4 tablespoons of the olive oil into a frying pan and get it hot, then fry the potatoes until tender and crispy. Then add the turmeric, and the remaining teaspoon of salt. Seed the chili, chop finely and add to the pan. Peel and crush the garlic cloves then add them. Cook for another 2–3 minutes.

6 Finally, add the cilantro leaves, coarsely chopped. When they have wilted in the heat, the potatoes are ready.

7 Roll the marinated herrings in the breadcrumbs and then panfry them in the remaining 2 tablespoons of olive oil until golden, turning once – for about 3 minutes a side, less if the fillets are small.

Shopping and showing off

Ask your fishmonger to fillet the herrings for you, and do try to get large ones as they have a better texture when cooked. To assemble the dish on the plate, start with a spoonful of the turmeric potatoes, then peel and slice the beets and arrange on top. Finally, add two herring fillets per person and a tablespoon of thick yogurt.

Hotpot of cod cheeks,
globe artichokes and button mushrooms
with potato bread and aïoli

This is a rich dish, and provides one occasion when you should certainly consider partnering fish with red wine. Serves four.

4 globe artichokes

1 lemon

2 garlic cloves

2 cups button mushrooms

2 cups sliced leeks

2 cups shallots

2 fat red chili peppers

$\frac{1}{2}$ bunch basil

$\frac{1}{4}$ cup olive oil

$\frac{3}{4}$ cup white wine

$\frac{3}{4}$ cup water

hearts of 2 heads frisée

about 1 pound fish (see Shopping and showing off)

salt and pepper

1 quantity Aïoli (see page 190)

a loaf of Potato Bread (see page 155)

1 Prepare the artichokes. Take off two layers of leaves and then slice through horizontally. Trim back to reveal the hairy center and remove it with a teaspoon. Rub each trimmed heart with a lemon and keep in water, to which a squeeze of lemon has been added

2 Peel and crush the garlic and chop the mushrooms; peel the shallots (but leave them whole), chop and seed the chilis, tear up the basil leaves. Add them all, with the artichokes and leeks, to 2 tablespoons of the oil in the bottom of a heavy pot and cook on the stovetop until everything has taken on a good color.

3 Add the wine and water.

4 Trim back the frisée until you are left with the hearts. Add them to the pot, put the lid on and continue to cook over low heat, until the artichoke hearts are done (they should be soft – like potatoes ready for mashing).

5 Place the rest of the oil in a frying pan and add the fish pieces to firm them up.

6 Use a slotted spoon to transfer the cod cheeks to the pot. Add them to the vegetables and put the lid on. Take off the heat immediately and leave to stand for 10 minutes.

Shopping and showing off

In practice, cod cheeks are those medallions of meat left near the rear of the head when the fillets have been taken off. They are becoming increasingly hard to find as fishmongers give way to freezer cabinets and fishmongery becomes a dying art. For this recipe you need 12 small lumps of firm fish. The meat around a cod's gills, or skate knobs, or even chunks of monkfish all work well. To present on the plate, take an artichoke heart from the pot and use it as a base, top with a spoonful of the Aïoli and pile a few ladlefuls of the hot pot on top. Serve with a slice of toasted Potato Bread or a thick slice of whole grain bread.

Broiled red mullet

with gigandaes plaki and tapenade

This dish miraculously seems to add up to more than the sum of its parts. The red mullet is simply treated but remains wonderfully firm and meaty; gigandaes plaki, a splendid bean dish, is very traditional – at least in Greece – and the tapenade offers an additional strong flavor. Serves four.

4 fillets red mullet, each weighing 6 ounces

a little light olive oil

sea salt

1 quantity Gigandaes Plaki (see page 24)

1 quantity of Tapenade (see page 184)

1 Brush the fillets with a little olive oil and sprinkle with sea salt for seasoning and some crunch.

2 Cook under a hot broiler until the fish is firm – about 3 minutes a side, skin side first. When pressed, accurately cooked fish should feel solid and springy rather than yielding.

Shopping and showing off

The most difficult thing about this dish is getting your hands on the right kind of red mullet. At Livebait we put this dish on the menu only when there are large red mullet available. These provide the right kind of substantial meaty fillet – the little fish known as "rougets" won't really do. If you cannot find the right red mullet, substitute other mullet fillets, or even monkfish fillets – although more delicately flavored fish may be swamped by the gigandaes plaki and tapenade combo. Serve in soup bowls or deep plates: a sea of beans with a fish fillet on top, crowned with a spoonful of Tapenade.

Roast cod with couscous crust

served with a chickpea, red wine and black pudding stew

The combination of the fresh-tasting, firm and flaky cod with the rich and earthy chickpea stew is a winner. Serves four.

$\frac{1}{3}$ cup couscous

juice of 1 orange

2 tablespoons good olive oil

4 (8 ounce) cod fillets, cut from the thick end

1 quantity Chickpea, Red Wine and Black Pudding Stew (see page 32)

1 Half cook the couscous in boiling water – this will take about 10 minutes – and drain.

2 Preheat your oven to 400°F.

3 Warm the orange juice in a nonreactive saucepan, add the couscous and the oil, stir, cover the pot with plastic wrap and put to one side in a warm place for an hour or more.

4 Place the cod pieces, skin side down, on a greased baking sheet, brush with a little oil and season well with salt and pepper. Add a thick – $\frac{1}{2}$-inch – crust of couscous. Cook in the oven for 8–10 minutes. If you like a particularly crispy crust, finish under a hot broiler until browned.

Shopping and showing off

If you use quick-cooking couscous, which is available from supermarkets, omit the initial parboiling stage. Thick cod is best for this dish, which benefits from simple presentation – a soup bowl full of stew topped with a piece of fish.

Broiled polenta cake,

roast tomatoes and tsatsiki

The polenta cake and the roast tomatoes can be prepared the day before, then finished off when you require them. This is both filling and delicious. Serves six hungry people or eight as a starter.

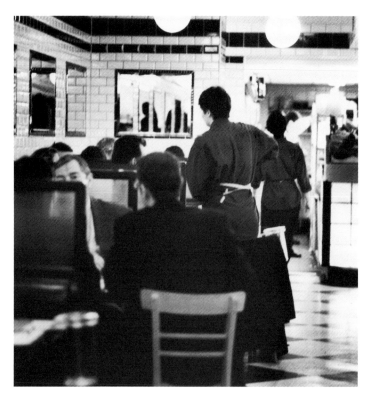

1 cup (1 ounce) dried porcini mushrooms

2 tablespoons dry white vermouth

6 plum tomatoes

salt and pepper

1 tablespoon dried thyme

3 garlic cloves

$\frac{1}{3}$ cup good olive oil

1 cucumber

1 cup yogurt

1 carrot

1 small fennel bulb

1 cup medium dry white wine

$4\frac{1}{4}$ cups water

$2\frac{1}{2}$ cups instant polenta

12 large cooked shrimp

2 ounces Parma ham

6 mussels

2 ounces Parmesan cheese

1 Preheat your oven to 210°F.

2 Put the porcini mushrooms to soak in the vermouth.

3 Slice the tomatoes in half, arrange them on a baking sheet and sprinkle with sea salt and thyme. Peel two of the garlic cloves and cut each into six slices. Put a slice on top of each tomato half. Drizzle with a tablespoon of olive oil. Put into the oven for an hour.

4 Remove and turn over each tomato with a spatula. Return to the oven for another hour.

5 Make the tsatsiki. Peel and seed the cucumber, then dice it very finely. Crush and chop the remaining garlic finely. Add both to the yogurt. Stir in a tablespoon of the olive oil and season with salt and pepper. Put to one side while the flavors amalgamate.

6 Peel, then chop the carrots finely. Chop the fennel finely. Cook them slowly with the lid on in the wine with 2 tablespoons of the olive oil, and a seasoning of salt and pepper. They should cook for 30 minutes.

7 Add the porcini and any vermouth that hasn't been soaked up. Cook for a further 30 minutes still leaving the lid on.

8 Bring the water to a boil with 1 tablespoon of salt. Add the polenta and stir it continuously as it thickens up and becomes a smooth porridge.

9 Chop the shrimp coarsely, and chop the Parma ham. Add them and the mussels, the braised vegetables, the Parmesan and the remaining olive oil to the mixture, stirring continually.

10 Take it off the heat, and when all is evenly mixed, pour it into a tray. The polenta should be no more than $\frac{3}{4}$ inch deep. Put the tray into the refrigerator to cool and solidify.

11 When ready to serve, cut the polenta cake into portions 3 inches square and crisp the top under a broiler.

Shopping and showing off

Use the polenta cake as a foundation for two tomato halves and a dollop of tsatsiki. Always be careful with leftover tsatsiki: the longer you leave it the more acrid the garlic flavor becomes.

John Dory, spinach and potato pie
with Pernod sauce

This pie makes a fine family dish – serve it with mashed potatoes. At Livebait, a debate continues over whether this pie goes best with the Pernod Sauce (see page 194) or with another sauce – try the Cumin Sauce (see page 197). Serves four.

1 sweet red pepper

1 sweet yellow pepper

$\frac{1}{2}$ pound spinach

$\frac{1}{2}$ pound potatoes

2 cups Chicken Stock (see page 188)

$\frac{1}{2}$ pound leeks

2 tablespoons olive oil

2 eggs

$\frac{1}{4}$ cup heavy cream

a bunch of fresh tarragon

1 pound John Dory fillets

$\frac{3}{4}$ cup flour

8 sheets from a pack of phyllo pastry

4 tablespoons melted butter

salt and pepper

1 quantity Pernod Sauce (see page 194)

1 Preheat your oven to 425 °F.

2 Cut in half and seed the peppers, then roast them briefly (5 minutes) in the oven. Remove and place in a sealed plastic bag. Rub off their skins when cool and wash under running water. Cut into wide strips. Turn the oven down to 325°F.

3 Wilt the spinach in boiling water, strain and reserve.

4 Peel the potatoes, then slice them very thinly, preferably with a mandoline. Heat the chicken stock in a pan and blanch the potatoes for 8–10 minutes, adding them a few at a time so that they do not clump together. Remove them from the liquid and reserve.

5 Chop the leeks finely, then cook in a little oil until soft.

6 Beat the eggs together and set some aside to use as egg wash. Add the cream to the remainder, strip the tarragon leaves from the stalks and stir into the mixture.

continued overleaf

7 Line an 8-inch springform cake pan with four sheets of phyllo pastry, each brushed with melted butter before the next is added.

8 Roll the fillets in flour and sear them in a pan with a little oil.

9 Fill the pie. Start with two or three layers of potato – seasoning each layer with salt and pepper – then peppers and leeks – mix the colors – then a layer of spinach, then two fish fillets. At this point pour on half the egg and cream mix. Top with two sheets of phyllo, glued together with melted butter.

10 Repeat stage 9.

11 Fold in the overhanging edges of phyllo, and brush with egg wash.

12 Bake for 50–60 minutes: the top should be nicely browned. Remove. Let stand for 5 minutes and take from the pan.

Shopping and showing off

Once again, we are looking for a helpful fishmonger to fillet the John Dory. If unavailable, you could substitute other thick white boneless fish fillets – cod, halibut or even pollock. Serve in a pool of Pernod Sauce.

Tuna with honey-roast chicken wings

and lentil stew

This is a dish that makes much of contrasts: there's the lean and solid tuna, the rich chicken wing meat and the earthy lentils. These multilayered tastes and textures are all too often the sole preserve of restaurant kitchens, but there's nothing challenging about the techniques involved: follow a succession of simple steps and reap the rewards yourself. Serves four.

$^1/_4$ cup honey

juice of $^1/_2$ a lemon

2 tablespoons dry white wine

2 teaspoons paprika

6-inch sprig rosemary

2 tablespoons olive oil

8 chicken wings

2 tablespoons Angostura bitters

2 tablespoons Worcestershire sauce

$1^1/_4$ pounds tuna loin

Salt and pepper

1 quantity Lentil Stew (see page 201)

1 Preheat your oven to 400°F.

2 Dissolve the honey into the lemon juice and white wine. Rub it into the chicken wings with the paprika and the leaves torn from the rosemary sprig.

3 Heat the oil in an ovenproof pan and seal the chicken wings. Do not let them burn.

4 Transfer the pan to the oven and cook for about 20 minutes, basting occasionally, until the meat is falling off the bone.

5 Shred the meat from the bone and mix with the Angostura and the Worcestershire sauce. Reserve in a warm place.

6 Trim the tuna and cut into four portions. Season well with salt and pepper and sear in a dry pan: it should be cooked on the outside and very rare inside.

7 Be sure the lentils are heated through before you serve them.

Shopping and showing off

You could substitute another thick and meatlike fish such as swordfish. Line the plates with lentils, then add the chicken meat and finally the tuna. Serve with a green salad.

Seared sea scallops with red wine pears

This dish looks amazing. The red wine pears have been rescued from their role on the dessert menu. Their spicing is changed and they are teamed with sweet scallops. The red wine juices are turned into a rich sauce. What's more, it is all very simple to do. Serves four.

4 hard pears

3 cloves

2 cinnamon sticks

peel from 1 large orange

$\frac{1}{4}$ cup brown sugar

$1\frac{1}{2}$ cups red wine

8 sea scallops – the larger the better

4 tablespoons chilled butter, plus a little extra

salt and pepper

1 Peel the pears and leave them whole.

2 In a nonreactive saucepan, add the cloves, cinnamon, sugar and orange peel to the red wine. Then add the pears, cover the pan, and poach gently until cooked (when they are soft to a knife). Remove and keep in a warm place. Strain the cooking liquid and reserve.

3 Smear a heavy frying pan with a minimum of butter. Heat it up and sear the scallops until cooked on the outside but not overcooked – they should be firm. Keep in a warm place.

4 Strain the cooking liquid and reduce, if need be, to $\frac{1}{2}$ cup (if cooking the pears has left you short of this amount, add a little more red wine). Take the butter straight from the refrigerator so that it is chilled, and cut it into cubes. Whisk it into the sauce which will thicken and become glossy. Adjust the seasoning with salt and pepper.

Shopping and showing off

Ask your fishmonger to clean and prepare the scallops for you. Serve simply in a pool of sauce with the pear sitting upright and the scallops sliced in half around it.

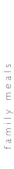

Fisherman's soup

There has been a great deal written about fish soup, and what started out as a simple dish has acquired enough mystique to become thoroughly daunting. The Livebait philosophy is to take the freshest ingredients, then allow their natural flavors and textures free rein. This recipe is your key to making a genuine fish soup with the minimum of fuss. As the recipe is a succession of simple steps, you don't have to be particularly skillful – just careful.

$^{1}/_{4}$ cup olive oil

1 head garlic, peeled and coarsely chopped

2 teaspoons fennel seeds

a bouquet garni, made with 8 sprigs flat parsley,

4 bay leaves, 6 celery leaves and 4 mint leaves tied together with fine string

2 teaspoons salt

freshly ground black pepper

$^{1}/_{3}$ cup tomato purée

18 ounces canned whole plum tomatoes

4 cups Fish Stock (see page 186)

2$^{1}/_{4}$ cups white wine

1 teaspoon paprika

2 small fennel bulbs

$^{3}/_{4}$ pound potatoes

juice and zest of $^{1}/_{2}$ orange

2 tablespoons Pernod

2$^{1}/_{4}$ pounds mixed white fish – monkfish, turbot, John Dory

1 teaspoon saffron

1 In a stockpot with a heavy bottom, heat the olive oil, add the garlic, fennel seeds, bouquet garni, and salt and pepper. Cook gently for 10 minutes.

2 Add the tomato purée, canned tomatoes, fish stock, wine and paprika. Bring to a boil and simmer, uncovered, for an hour.

3 Remove the bouquet garni and pass the soup through the coarsest blade of a food mill – as a second-best option process it in a food processor but do not allow it to become too fine. Return to the stockpot.

family meals

continued overleaf

4 Cut the fennel bulbs into quarters lengthwise. Peel the potatoes, then cut them into chunks. Add the fennel, the potatoes, the orange juice and zest, and the Pernod to the pot, then simmer until the potatoes are done – about 15 minutes.

5 Cut the fish into bite-sized chunks. Put the saffron into a small bowl with a little boiling water and steep for 2 minutes. Add the fish and saffron to the pot and simmer for 3–4 minutes until the fish is just cooked.

Shopping and showing off

Omit any single ingredient, except the saffron and the fish stock, and this soup will still be delicious, so feel free to adapt it to suit yourself. You can also pick and choose just which fish to use depending upon availability – after all, that is what fishermen do! Serve in a soup bowl with crusty bread (see pages 142–57), and if you are nostalgic for the south of France add a dollop of Aïoli (see page 190).

Seared salmon

with potato, cilantro and lemongrass dauphinoise, and an artichoke dressing

This takes a simply cooked fillet of salmon and partners it with a new kind of dauphinoise and a chunky artichoke dressing which is particularly good. Serves four.

1 globe artichoke

$\frac{1}{2}$ lemon

5 teaspoons smooth Dijon mustard

$\frac{1}{4}$ cup light olive oil

5 teaspoons balsamic vinegar

salt and pepper

4 (4-ounce) salmon fillets

1 teaspoon clarified butter

1 quantity Potato, Cilantro and Lemongrass Dauphinoise (see page 203)

1 First prepare the artichoke. Take off two layers of leaves and then slice through horizontally. Trim back to reveal the hairy choke in the center and remove it with a teaspoon. Rub the trimmed heart all over with half a lemon.

2 Steam the artichoke heart over boiling water until it is tender but not mushy.

3 Cut it into strips and put them in a food processor or blender with the mustard, oil and vinegar, and process until you have a chunky consistency, not a purée. Put the dressing into a small pan and warm gently. Season with salt and pepper.

4 Season the salmon fillets with salt and pepper and, using the clarified butter, sear them in a very hot frying pan. The fillets are done when the outside looks cooked but the very center is still raw. Take from the pan and allow to rest for 3 minutes before serving.

Shopping and showing off

The best salmon is wild salmon. Better texture. Better taste. But farmed salmon is both more widely available and a good deal cheaper – ask your fishmonger to do the filleting and to remove the pin bones. To bring out the best in this dish put the salmon in the center of the plate and spoon some of the artichoke dressing over it. Add a wedge of the dauphinoise or, if more bravura is called for, use a pastry cutter to ease out a perfect cylinder of the potatoes.

family meals

Broiled smoked sturgeon
with "nero" spinach and paprika sour cream

This stunning dish has just the right combination of textures and flavors, where green vegetables are braised in squid ink and red wine to form a backdrop to plainly broiled fish. So, no . . . you cannot make any substitutions. Serves four.

1 cup finely sliced leeks (white parts only)

$1/4$ cup good olive oil

12 ounces young spinach leaves

$3\frac{1}{2}$ ounces curly endive leaves

$1/2$ cup Chicken Stock (see page 188)

$1/2$ cup red wine

$1/4$ cup squid ink

salt and pepper

$1/2$ cup sour cream

1 tablespoon sweet paprika

4 (4-ounce) pieces smoked sturgeon

2 tablespoons butter

2 tablespoons salmon "caviar" (optional)

1 Soften the leeks in the oil in a heavy pan. Do not allow them to color.

2 Wash the spinach and the curly endive (use only the white part). Add them to the pan with the chicken stock and red wine. Braise with the lid on for 30 minutes.

3 Add the squid ink and braise for a further 15 minutes. Take the lid off and stir – the contents should be nearly dry; if still sloppy cook a little longer with the lid off. Season with salt and pepper and keep warm.

4 Mix the sour cream with the paprika and reserve.

5 Butter the sturgeon portions. Cook under a hot broiler for 4–5 minutes.

Shopping and showing off

The "nero" vegetable braise is so original that it makes a good partner for any plainly broiled fish. If you can find the paprika powder made from smoked peppers, use it. To serve, start with a foundation of greens, then top with a piece of fish and a dollop of the paprika sour cream. A sprinkling of salmon "caviar" as garnish adds another element of color.

Roast monkfish tail

with braised red cabbage

This is comfort food, and about as unfussy as you can get: when it went on the menu at Livebait there was a constant procession of customers asking for the red cabbage recipe. As for all those people who know in their hearts that they should be eating more fish – yes, fish is good for the brain! – this recipe makes a great starting point. It just needs a little mashed potato with it to take care of the juices from the braised red cabbage. Serves four.

6 tablespoons good olive oil

1 bunch fresh tarragon

1½ pounds boned and trimmed monkfish tail

salt and pepper

¼ pound (1 stick) unsalted butter

1 cup shallots

½ cup celery leaves

½ cup flat-leafed parsley

2 bay leaves

1 tablespoon snipped thyme

1 red cabbage

1 scant cup red wine

½ cup freshly squeezed orange juice

1 scant cup Chicken Stock (see page 188)

3 tablespoons brown sugar

6 ounces unsmoked bacon

½ cup pitted prunes

3 tablespoons sherry vinegar

1 Make up a marinade from 3 tablespoons of the good olive oil and half the tarragon. Season the monkfish with salt and pepper, then roll it in the marinade. Put to one side for 30 minutes.

2 Put the remaining 3 tablespoons of good olive oil and the butter into a nonreactive casserole dish – one that will take direct heat – peel and quarter the shallots and add them with the celery leaves, the rest of the tarragon, the parsley, bay leaves and thyme. Stir until mixed and then put on the lid, turn down the heat very low and cook, covered, for 10 minutes.

3 Preheat your oven to 425°F.

4 Chop the cabbage coarsely and add it to the pot. Add the red wine, orange juice, chicken stock and sugar. Stir and braise for another 40 minutes with the lid on.

5 Brown the outside of the monkfish in a roasting tray. Take the bacon slices and stretch them out using the back of a knife. Wrap them around the sealed monkfish tail. Then roast it for about 25 minutes.

6 Chop the prunes, then add with the sherry vinegar to the cabbage and braise for a further 15 minutes with the lid off. Remove the bay leaves. Taste and adjust seasoning with salt and pepper.

Shopping and showing off

Ask your fishmonger to skin and bone the monkfish tail, although this is a job you can do at home. The dish goes well with some mashed potatoes, so to present the dish, start with a foundation of mashed potatoes and red cabbage, then slice the monkfish tail neatly and place three slices on each plate — it's as simple as that.

grandstand
dishes

Smoked fish terrine *(see opposite)* **84**   Roast fillet of turbot with foie gras mashed potatoes, braised celery and red wine sauce 86   **Risotto cake with smoked trout, sauce gribiche and roast radicchio 88**   "Millefeuille" of seared bluefin tuna, baba ganoush, red onion jam and baby spinach 90   **Baked whole porgy stuffed with couscous tabbouleh and served with a potato and hazelnut gratin 92**   Tiger shrimp wrapped in sea bass and roasted, with egg tagliatelle, mussels and Merguez sausage 94   **Roast turbot with brandade mashed potatoes and Champagne porcini sauce 96**   Tart of mussels in a red curry paste 100   **Crab and wild mushrooms on brioche toast with foie gras vinaigrette 102**   Oysters and caramelized leeks, with Champagne and strawberry hollandaise sauce 104

Smoked fish terrine

This terrine is beautiful to look at, delicious to eat and tricky to make. Preparing it is quite laborious, but doesn't involve any particularly difficult techniques or obscure ingredients. Take your time, do the job step by step, and you will be delighted with the results. This makes approximately 4½ pounds of terrine – you'll need a mold about 12 inches long, with a capacity of about 9 cups, and you'll end up with enough terrine for at least twelve large portions.

4 red bell peppers

4 zucchini

1 tablespoon light olive oil

juice of ½ lemon

1¼ pounds potatoes

3¼ cups Fish Stock (see page 186) *or* water

bunch of flat-leafed parsley

¼ ounce gelatin

1 pound smoked haddock

1 pound smoked eel

1 pound smoked salmon

salt and pepper

2 quantities Horseradish Cream (see page 192)

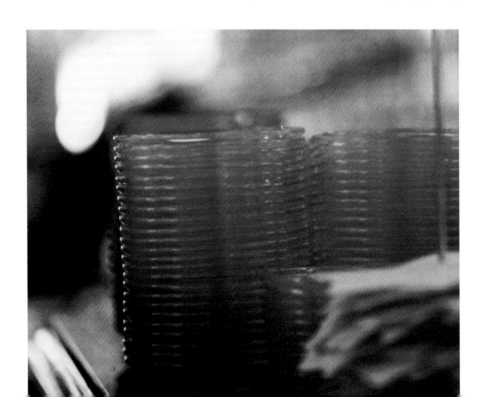

1 Preheat your oven to 400°F.

2 First things first — preparations. The peppers should be split in half and seeded, then roasted in the oven until just softening — about 20 minutes. Remove and place in a sealed plastic bag. When cool, pull off the skins and cut the peppers into strips about ¾ inch wide.

3 Slice the zucchini thinly lengthwise. Brush with a little oil and lemon juice, then soften in the oven for about 10 minutes. Allow to cool.

4 Peel and slice the potatoes thinly lengthwise, then parboil them in fish stock — they should still be "crunchy."

5 Strip the parsley leaves from their stems and reserve.

6 Make up the gelatin with hot water, or a little of the potato water, and put to one side.

7 Take the terrine, oil it lightly, and line it carefully with a sheet of plastic wrap that hangs over the edges. This will make turning it out much less of an ordeal.

8 Cut your smoked fish into 2-inch slices, working along their length, but at a 45-degree angle as if you were slicing smoked salmon.

9 Remember to season the vegetable layers with salt and pepper as you go; the fish layers just require pepper.

10 Build stage one in the terrine: a layer of smoked haddock; one of peppers; one of potatoes; one of zucchini; one of parsley. Seal with a third of the gelatin mixture and place in the refrigerator for 20 minutes.

11 Build stage two on top: a layer of smoked eel; one of peppers; one of potatoes; one of zucchini; one of parsley. Seal with another third of the gelatin mixture and once again place in the refrigerator for 20 minutes.

12 Finally, build stage three: a layer of smoked salmon; one of peppers; one of potatoes; one of zucchini; one of parsley. Seal with the last of the gelatin mixture. Fold over the plastic wrap and place in the refrigerator overnight to set firm.

Shopping and showing off

Smoked wild salmon is preferable to farmed. If you cannot find smoked eel, substitute smoked mackerel. When you have turned out the terrine, slice it with a serrated knife into elegant slices and arrange each on a plate with some green salad leaves and a dollop of Horseradish Cream.

Roast fillet of turbot
with foie gras mashed potatoes, braised celery and red wine sauce

Turbot is the king of fish, with solid, uncompromising flesh that is so rich as to taste almost creamy. Finding a combination of vegetables and a sauce that goes well with such a fish is a taxing problem. This plateful really sings, though the opulent mashed potatoes, the slightly crunchy celery and the rich red wine sauce are all great on their own. With the turbot they are even better. Serves four.

1⅔ cups (1¾ ounces) dried porcini mushrooms

3 cups rich red wine

6 cups Chicken Stock (see page 188)

12 celery stalks

2¼ pounds floury potatoes

4 (12-ounce) turbot fillets

¼ cup good olive oil

⅓ cup sweet white wine

3½ ounces fresh foie gras, prepared by your supplier

¼ cup heavy cream

4 tablespoons butter

salt and pepper

1 Soak the porcini with 1 cup of the red wine for 60 minutes

2 Preheat the oven to 425°F.

3 Take 4 cups of the chicken stock and boil until reduced by half. Reserve.

4 Take the remaining 2 cups of red wine and boil until reduced by half.

5 Drain the porcini mushrooms, and pass the red wine they were soaking in through a cloth to remove any grit.

6 Amalgamate the reduced stock, the reduced wine, the mushrooms and the wine they were soaked in. Simmer together for 30–40 minutes.

7 Peel the celery stalks to remove the strings and cut into 1-inch lengths. Put them in a saucepan with the remaining 2 cups of chicken stock, add a teaspoon of salt and cook slowly until they are just done but still a little crunchy. Reserve.

8 Peel and boil the potatoes until they are cooked. Drain and keep warm.

9 Season the turbot fillets with salt and pepper, and brush with a little olive oil. Sear in a frying pan to seal, then transfer to a heated roasting dish. Finish in the oven for about 8 minutes. The fish is done when it feels firm and resilient to the touch.

10 Put the sweet white wine into a saucepan and reduce until there are only a couple of tablespoons left. If the foie gras is raw, add it and heat through for 2 minutes. If the foie gras is cooked, take the pan off the heat and then add it.

11 Mash the potatoes with the cream and butter. Add the foie gras and sweet wine from the saucepan and mash to mix well. Season to taste.

Shopping and showing off

For this dish the larger the turbot fillets the better; twice as many small ones is not really an option. If you cannot get fresh foie gras, then it is more readily available in tins and jars; unfortunately it is no less expensive. Finely chopped chicken livers will do as a last resort substitute. To present the dish, start with an island of mashed potatoes surrounded by a sea of mushroom and red wine sauce, top with the fish fillet and finally the celery.

grandstand dishes

87

Risotto cake with smoked trout,
sauce gribiche and roast radicchio

At last, a risotto with crispy bits! Panfrying risotto is a sure way to combine the best of both worlds: on one hand there is the creamy center and on the other there is that bit of crunch. Plus this dish delivers the winning combination of sweet-fleshed smoked trout and bitter radicchio. At Livebait the risotto cakes are made individually in small ring molds and then pushed out as perfect circles. In the home it is easier to make one large cake in a frying pan; then you have the option of punching out a perfect disc of risotto with a pastry cutter (and of saving the risotto trimmings to eat the following day – just stir them back to life with a little fresh stock) or you can cut the cake into simple wedges. Serves four.

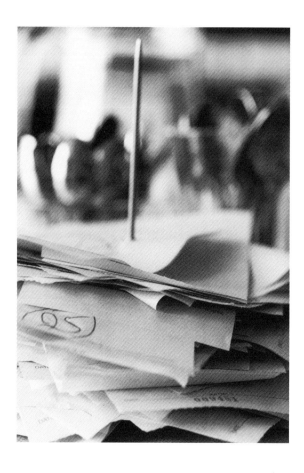

¾ cup finely diced red onion

¾ cup finely diced sweet yellow pepper

⅓ cup olive oil

I pound Italian risotto rice

⅓ cup white wine

I small bunch tarragon

¾ cup grated Parmesan

3 cups Chicken Stock (see page 188)

I egg

¼ cup heavy cream

salt and pepper

4 small heads radicchio

4 small smoked trout

I quantity Sauce Gribiche (see page 194)

1 Preheat your oven to 400°F.

2 Cook the onion and pepper in a deep saucepan with $\frac{1}{4}$ cup of the olive oil until soft. Add the rice and cook for a minute or two.

3 Add the wine and stir until it is all absorbed.

4 Warm the chicken stock and stir into the rice mixture a ladleful at a time, only proceeding when the previous quantity has been absorbed.

5 When all the stock is incorporated take the pan off the heat and allow to cool down.

6 Beat the Parmesan with the egg and the cream. Stir into the risotto, which should end up quite firm, not sloppy.

7 Peel the radicchio to leave neat hearts, brush with oil and roast in the oven for 10 minutes.

8 Transfer the risotto mixture to a deep frying pan and cook until a good crisp skin has formed. Lift the edge of the cake up with a spatula to check.

9 Then put the pan under a hot broiler to crisp up the top of the cake.

10 Turn the trout over on their backs and, using scissors, snip through the backbone just by the head and just by the tail – you should be able to pull the bone free (and all the pin bones should come with it), leaving a boneless fish that still has its head and tail.

Shopping and showing off

You can use any medium-grain rice, but a genuine risotto rice like arborio or carnoli is preferable. If you don't want to go so far as the "head and tail" presentation outlined here, smoked trout fillets will suffice. Cut the risotto cake into four wedges. Place one on a plate and top with a trout. Surround with Sauce Gribiche, then garnish with a roasted radicchio head split into four.

"Millefeuille" of seared bluefin tuna,

baba ganoush, red onion jam and baby spinach

This makes a fine dinner party starter, fish course or even centerpiece. Make the "biscuit" element of the millefeuille in whatever size and shape suits your presentation but remember that, in the home kitchen, larger is generally easier. Both the Baba Ganoush and the Red Onion Jam need to be prepared ahead of time. The recipe serves four, based on four "biscuits" each, when each biscuit is about 2 inches square.

1 pound frozen puff pastry, or phyllo dough

1 egg

1 pound bluefin tuna loin

salt and pepper

$\frac{1}{2}$ pound baby spinach

2 tablespoons good olive oil

1 quantity Baba Ganoush (see page 198–9)

1 quantity Red Onion Jam (see page 182)

watercress to garnish

1 Preheat your oven to 400°F.

2 Start by making the "biscuits." Roll out the puff pastry until it is 1 inch thick. Mark out into 16 biscuits with the back of a knife, scoring the pastry fairly deeply but not cutting right through it.

3 Beat the egg and use it to glaze the biscuits. Then arrange them on a baking sheet lined with baking parchment.

3 Bake in the oven for 15–20 minutes. Cool on a rack, then cut into biscuits.

4 Heat a frying pan with just the merest dab of oil. Season the tuna with salt and pepper, then sear it on all sides. It should be cooked on the outside and raw in the middle.

5 Cut the seared tuna into 12 equal slices.

6 To assemble: put a tiny smear of Baba Ganoush on the plate to glue everything in place, and add a pastry biscuit glazed side up; then take one of the tuna slices, brush with olive oil and lay out on the biscuit; then a few leaves of spinach; then a biscuit; then a tuna slice brushed with oil; then a layer of Red Onion Jam; then a biscuit; then a tuna slice brushed with oil; then a layer of Baba Ganoush; then a final biscuit, glazed side up. Watercress makes the best garnish.

Shopping and showing off

If your fishmonger doesn't have any bluefin tuna you could substitute fresh raw salmon – it's worth getting wild salmon if you can, as the texture is so much better. If you find yourself making the Red Onion Jam and Baba Ganoush just for this recipe, the Bread section (see pages 142–57) will help you use up any surplus.

grandstand dishes

91

Baked whole porgy
stuffed with couscous tabbouleh and served with a potato and hazelnut gratin

The porgy is a tasty and much underrated fish, and serving an individual fish to each diner is certainly a showstopper. Serves four.

1 cup couscous

juice of 1 orange

6 tablespoons olive oil, plus a little extra

½ sweet red pepper

½ sweet yellow pepper

½ bunch scallions

2 plum tomatoes

1 zucchini

1 cucumber

salt and pepper

2 teaspoons hot chili paste

4 (12-ounce) porgies

1 quantity Potato and Hazelnut Gratin (see page 38)

watercress or leaves to garnish

grandstand dishes

1 Preheat your oven to 400°F.

2 Half-cook the couscous in boiling salted water – this will take about 10 minutes.

3 Warm the orange juice in a nonreactive saucepan, add the couscous and $\frac{1}{4}$ cup of olive oil, stir, cover the pot with plastic wrap and put to one side in a warm place for an hour or more.

4 Prepare all the vegetables. To skin the peppers, toast them under a broiler until black, then leave in a sealed plastic bag until cool – the skins will rub off; then dice. Chop the scallions; peel, seed and chop the tomatoes; dice the zucchini; peel, seed and dice the cucumber.

5 Season the vegetable mix, then dissolve the chili paste in the remaining 2 tablespoons of olive oil and drizzle over the vegetables.

6 Crumble the couscous by hand and mix with the vegetables.

7 Take each fish and use scissors to snip through the backbone close to the head and again at the tail. Press down on the bone, then pull away the backbone and the pin bones. Stuff the cavity with the couscous mixture and "stitch" up the belly with a thin, oiled bamboo or steel skewer.

8 Oil the fish, then season with salt and pepper and roast for 25 minutes in a hot oven. Serve with Potato and Hazelnut Gratin.

Shopping and showing off

Use a concentrated hot chili paste. Plate each fish and garnish with watercress or other dark green leaves. Place a wedge of Potato and Hazelnut Gratin to one side.

Tiger shrimp wrapped in sea bass
and roasted, with egg tagliatelle, mussels and Merguez sausage

This dish looks good and tastes good too. The egg tagliatelle with mussels and Merguez sausage makes it substantial and there is an invaluable "surprise" spicy flavor in the lurking Merguez sausage. If you cannot find Merguez (a spicy, fatty lamb sausage) use another spicy sausage, such as hot pepperoni. Serves four.

4 extra large raw tiger shrimp

4 ($\frac{1}{2}$-pound) sea bass fillets

2 tablespoons olive oil

salt and pepper

I quantity Egg Tagliatelle with Mussels and Merguez Sausage (see page 40)

1 Preheat your oven to 335°F.

2 Carefully peel the tail part of the shell from the shrimp, being careful to leave the head attached. Run a knife down the back of each shrimp to remove the dark vein.

3 Season the sea bass fillets with salt and pepper and wrap each one carefully round the tail of a shrimp – leaving the head poking out, as if the shrimp were in a giant sleeping bag. Secure the parcel with a toothpick to prevent it unraveling. Brush with olive oil.

4 Place upright on a baking sheet and roast in the oven for 8–10 minutes.

Shopping and showing off

Tiger shrimp are sometimes available, or you can substitute *very* large shrimp – failing these you can substitute langostinos but they must be raw. In a pinch, you could use small lobster tails. Ask your fishmonger to fillet and pin-bone the sea bass. To serve, simply position your shrimp-crowned fillet on the top of a hillock of the tagliatelle.

Roast turbot with brandade mashed potatoes and Champagne porcini sauce

Turbot is a very finely flavored fish, and the rich and substantial Brandade Mashed Potatoes (see page 26) suits it very well, as does the Champagne porcini sauce. Serves four.

1 cup dried porcini

1 quantity Brandade Mashed Potatoes (see page 26)

$\frac{1}{3}$ cup shallots

2 tablespoons light olive oil

1 bunch fresh tarragon

2 cups Chicken Stock (see page 188)

1 cup Champagne

$\frac{1}{3}$ cup heavy cream

1 (3$\frac{1}{2}$–4$\frac{1}{2}$ pound) turbot, filleted

salt and pepper

1 Cover the porcini in warm water and leave them to rehydrate for at least an hour.

2 Preheat your oven to 425°F.

3 If you are using leftover Brandade Mashed Potatoes, put them into a gratin dish and place in the bottom of the oven to warm through.

4 Chop the shallots and cook slowly, covered, in a little of the oil. Drain the mushrooms, saving the water but straining it through a cloth to remove any grit. Then add the mushrooms to the pan. Fry everything together for 3–4 minutes.

5 Add the mushroom water and reduce by half.

6 Strip the tarragon leaves from their stalks and add them. Add the stock and reduce by half.

7 Add ¾ cup of the Champagne and reduce by half.

8 Add the cream and reduce until the sauce coats the back of a spoon.

9 Take off the heat and keep warm.

10 Season the turbot fillets and seal on both sides in a hot pan with a little oil.

11 Roast in the oven for 6–7 minutes. They are cooked when resilient to the touch.

12 Meanwhile finish the sauce: add the remaining Champagne, stir and adjust the seasoning.

Shopping and showing off

If you balk at cooking with Champagne (despite the fact you get a cast-iron excuse to drink the remaining four glasses from the bottle), domestic bubbly will do fine. Pompano can be used as a substitute for turbot. Serve by piling a mound of the wonderful Brandade Mashed Potatoes centrally, topping it with a turbot fillet and adding a moat of Champagne Porcini Sauce.

Tart of mussels in a red curry paste

This is a Thai-inspired red curry paste and, as with all curry pastes, its exact composition is subject to the availability of the various ingredients. At Livebait we use more chilis, and add some cilantro root, which gives a very concentrated flavor. Take the recipe here and use it as a starting point for your own experiments. These quantities will make two 8-inch tarts, which will serve eight.

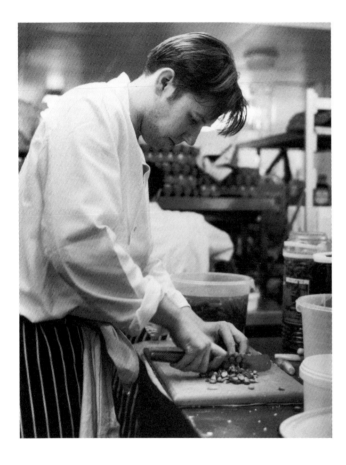

1½ heads garlic

4 ounces red onions

6 tablespoons powdered galangal

4 ounces lemongrass

3 fat red chili peppers

juice of 2 limes

4 tablespoons "blachan" – shrimp paste

1 teaspoon powdered cinnamon

1 teaspoon pink peppercorns

1 teaspoon cumin seeds

1 teaspoon coriander powder

1 teaspoon sweet paprika

¼ cup coconut milk

¼ cup sake *or* dry sherry

¼ cup (just over 2 ounces) sweet potato

1¾ pounds mussel meat

1 bunch fresh cilantro

6 tablespoons crème fraîche

2 eggs

2 frozen 8-inch pie shells

1 Preheat your oven to 350°F.

2 Peel and chop the garlic, onions, lemongrass and chilis. Then add them with the galangal, lime juice, shrimp paste and spices to a food processor or blender. While the machine is running, add enough water (⅓ cup or so) to make a paste.

3 Put the paste into a pan and heat gently. Add the coconut milk and sake and reduce by half.

4 Blind bake the pie shells by putting a sheet of greased baking parchment into each, and weighting it with dried beans. Put them in the oven for 15 minutes. Remove, discard the paper and beans, brush the inside with beaten egg and return to the oven for 5 minutes. The tarts are then ready for their filling.

5 Peel and dice the sweet potato and cook gently in the sauce until done (about 20 minutes).

6 Chop the cilantro leaves. Add the mussels and cilantro to the cooling red sauce mix.

7 Beat the crème fraîche with the eggs and stir into the mix.

8 Fill the pie shells with the mixture and return them to the oven for 30 minutes.

Shopping and showing off

Anything you do not immediately recognize on the ingredients list can probably be found at any shop specializing in Thai food or in a mail order catalog from a spice company. And such has been the recent surge in popularity of Thai dishes that many of the large supermarkets will have them too. You may prefer to make a number of individual tartlets rather than two large tarts, but either way a salad of crisp green leaves makes the perfect accompaniment. Mussel meat (no shells) can be found in most fish stores; if you have to buy whole mussels in their shells, let the store calculate the quantity you will need.

Crab and wild mushrooms

on brioche toast with foie gras vinaigrette

This is an assemblage, but a very cunning one. The crab is very rich, and the mushrooms provide a different texture – as does the toast. Let the wild mushrooms be chanterelles, although whatever your supermarket can supply, up to and including reconstituted porcini, will do. Serves four.

1 quantity Foie Gras Vinaigrette (see page 192)

1 pink grapefruit

$1\frac{1}{2}$ cups finely chopped leeks, from the white part

$\frac{1}{4}$ cup good olive oil

$\frac{3}{4}$ pound fresh chanterelles *or* other wild mushrooms

$\frac{1}{4}$ cup dry white wine

1 bunch fresh tarragon

1 bunch scallions

1 pound white, hand-picked crab meat

salt and pepper

4 slices brioche

1 Make the Foie Gras Vinaigrette in advance and cut the grapefruit into segments, removing all pith and skin.

2 Soften the leeks in a heavy lidded pan, with the oil.

3 Brush the mushrooms to get rid of grit, chop them roughly and add them and the white wine to the casserole. Strip the tarragon leaves from the stems and add them.

4 Put on the lid, turn down to a simmer and cook for 15–20 minutes.

5 Finely chop the scallions and add, then stir in the crab. Adjust the seasoning, and keep warm.

6 Toast the brioche.

Shopping and showing off

One pound of picked crab meat is roughly what you would get from a $4\frac{1}{2}$ pound cock crab. By all means take a shortcut and get the crab ready-picked from your fishmonger, but do be sure that the crab meat is fresh. For presentation, start with a slice of brioche toast and top with the crab-and-mushroom mixture, then add the grapefruit segments. Dress with the Foie Gras Vinaigrette (see page 192). Either buy a brioche or make your own (see page 156), or even get away with a slice of good whole grain toast, well buttered.

Oysters and caramelized leeks,

with Champagne and strawberry hollandaise sauce

It's easy to forget how acidic strawberries are. In this dish they provide a welcome bite to a Champagne hollandaise sauce. The oysters are poached to firm them up, and the leeks cooked to bring out their sweetness. This is a great dish to show off with, but you do need a hand blender and a thermometer. Serves four.

2 cups finely chopped leeks, white parts only

$\frac{1}{2}$ small red chili pepper

4 tablespoons salted butter

6 strawberries

$\frac{1}{2}$ lemon

12 large oysters

$\frac{1}{3}$ cup white wine

$\frac{1}{3}$ cup Champagne

1 tablespoon white wine vinegar

1 teaspoon pickled green peppercorns

4 egg yolks

$\frac{1}{2}$ pound (2 sticks) lukewarm clarified butter

salt and pepper

1 Place the leeks in a saucepan with the salted butter. Seed and chop the red chili very finely and add it to the pan. Cook slowly for 30 minutes. The leeks should be reduced to a rich, caramelized mass. Reserve.

2 Make a strawberry purée in your food processor: process the strawberries and adjust the taste with lemon juice.

3 Open the oysters (unless you have inveigled your fishmonger into doing this job for you! Remember to ask for the shells and juice).

4 Remove the meat and save the liquid from the oysters. Mix the oyster juice with the white wine and boil for 3 minutes until the alcohol has gone.

5 Allow to cool down to 160°F – check with a thermometer – then "poach" the oysters for 3 minutes without allowing the liquid to boil. Do not overcook and the oysters will stay plump. Remove and allow to cool.

grandstand dishes

6 Put the Champagne, vinegar and peppercorns in a saucepan and reduce over a low heat until you have about ¼ cup of liquid. Cool.

7 When cool add the egg yolks and use a hand blender to mix thoroughly. Put the saucepan on minimal heat and continue to blend. The sauce should grow in volume and become fluffy and light. Do NOT exceed 140°F or you will have scrambled eggs!

8 Remove from the stove, continue to blend and gradually add the cool clarified butter, then add the strawberry purée. Season with salt and pepper.

9 Take half of the deep oyster shells and fill each with: a layer of caramelized leek, 1 oyster meat, a thick coating of Champagne and strawberry hollandaise. Then finish under a hot broiler, being careful that the hollandaise doesn't burn.

Shopping and showing off

Opening oysters is easier than it looks: ask for a demo at the fishmonger's, get an oyster knife and start practicing. At Livebait, we serve three shells, which makes a good portion, and the dish is made even more extravagant by the addition of a dollop of Sevruga caviar.

dinners à deux

Tartare of home-salted cod, avocado and radish fool with an egg yolk *(see opposite)* 108   Tuna au poivre with Sichuan pickled cucumbers and black shiitake mushrooms 111   **Turbot with seared scallops and a casserole of summer vegetables 112**   Honey and ginger roast octopus 114 **Sea scallops with vegetable tagine 117**   Spring rolls of squid, oyster and bacon with chicory frisée and shiitake mushrooms, apple and raisin chutney 118   **Broiled salmon on an artichoke "pizza" with tomatoes and feta cheese 120**   Sea scallops with roast quince and cardoon 122 **Lobster, Yellow Finn potato salad with oyster mushrooms, salmon "caviar" and gazpacho sauce 124**

Tartare of home-salted cod, avocado and radish fool with an egg yolk

This dish provides a succession of contrasting textures. The avocado fool is a smooth green purée with chunks of peppery radish bobbing around like early naval mines, while the home-cured cod is firm and somehow tastes fresher than fresh! The only drawback is that the dish does need planning: it will never be the star of an impromptu meal. Serves two with cod left over – which is splendid in sandwiches or on toast.

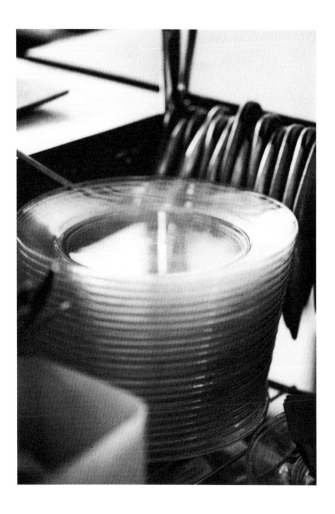

1 fat red chili pepper

1 bunch flat-leafed parsley

1 1/4 cups granulated sugar

5 tablespoons sea salt

2 1/4 pounds thick fillet of cod, pin-boned

1/2 cup heavy cream

juice of 1/2 lemon

1 ripe avocado

2 scallions

salt and pepper

1/2 bunch radishes

2 tablespoons good olive oil

2 egg yolks

1/2 cup cornichons

1/2 cup capers

1 teaspoon sweet paprika

1 To cure the cod: finely chop the chili and parsley, mix with the sugar and salt. Cover the bottom of a plastic container (one that has a lid) with a third of the mixture. Put the cod fillet on the salt mix, skin side down. Cover with the rest of the mixture. Leave for 24 hours with the lid on in the refrigerator (unless yours gets colder than 42°F – if the cod gets very cold it starts to freeze, which inhibits the curing process). Turn the fish once.

2 To make the fool, place the cream and lemon juice in your food processor – or blender – and process until the cream is whipped to stiff peaks. This is important as the whipped cream will give the fool its lightness.

3 Dice the avocado, chop the scallions and add them as you continue to process.

4 Season with salt and freshly ground black pepper.

5 Rinse the cod thoroughly and slice it as thinly as possible on the bias – in the same way that you would cut smoked salmon.

Shopping and showing off

Cod: make your fishmonger work for his money – you want it from the thick end and you want the pin bones removed. Eggs: it is still the advice of health agencies that we not eat raw eggs, which is a pity as the egg yolk lubricates the whole dish wonderfully. If you disagree with the official line and wish to take the responsibility on yourself, use really good fresh eggs that are free-range and come from a flock certified free of salmonella; otherwise omit the egg yolk. Start with a dollop of fool on each plate. Cut the radishes into quarters and embed them in the fool. Top with a fan of sliced cod. Paint with olive oil so that it glistens prettily and sit an unbroken egg yolk on the very top. Chop the cornichons and scatter them with the capers around the edges of the plate. Drizzle over some olive oil and use the paprika to add color.

Tuna au poivre

with Sichuan pickled cucumbers
and black shiitake mushrooms

Treating loin of tuna as if it were meat makes a lot of sense: it is solid, best eaten rare and carries a strong flavor well. Ask your fishmonger for a nice chunk of loin of tuna without the belly piece. Make the cucumber-and-mushroom pickle a day or two in advance, and this sophisticated dish comes together very quickly indeed. Serves two.

$\frac{1}{2}$ cup mixed peppercorns – green, black, pink and white

I pound loin of tuna

salt

a smear of light olive oil

I quantity Sichuan Pickled Cucumbers and Black Shiitake Mushrooms (see page 184)

1 Preheat your oven to 425°F.

2 Crack the peppercorns in a pestle and mortar or, failing that, use a coffee grinder. They need to be in small pieces but not turned to dust.

3 Salt the whole piece of tuna, then roll it in the peppercorn mixture – press the cracked pepper into the fish.

4 Get a heavy pan very hot and lubricate with a minimum of olive oil.

5 Press each surface of the tuna on to the hot pan. By the time you have finished, the fish will be almost cooked. Transfer to the oven for 2–3 minutes. The objective is for the tuna to remain very rare in the center.

6 Rest for a further 5 minutes, then slice.

Shopping and showing off

Buy tuna just as you would buy steak: it's expensive, it's a treat, it should be chosen and handled with care. Find a good fishmonger you can trust. Multicolored peppercorns may be found in mail order catalogs from a spice company, or from some specialty shops. To serve, arrange the slices of tuna carefully and surround with the Sichuan pickle.

Turbot with seared sea scallops
and a casserole of summer vegetables

A delicious dish, and one where you have some flexibility. Peas and broad beans form the basis for this casserole of fresh vegetables, but you could mix and match with other ingredients like artichoke hearts and asparagus. The casserole should be very sloppy and a foil for the solid turbot and tender scallops. Serves two.

$^1/_2$ pound shallots

3 garlic cloves

1 bunch fresh dill

$^1/_2$ bunch fresh parsley

$^1/_2$ cup good olive oil

3 plum tomatoes

$^1/_2$ pound fava beans in the pod *or* $^1/_4$ pound frozen

$^1/_2$ pound peas in the pod *or* $^1/_4$ pound frozen

1 artichoke heart (optional)

$1^1/_4$ cups water

juice of $^1/_2$ lemon

salt and pepper

$^1/_2$ pound asparagus spears (optional)

2 ($^1/_2$ pound) turbot fillets

6 tablespoons flour

$^1/_2$ cup light olive oil

4 large fresh sea scallops

1 bunch fresh basil

1 Peel the shallots and leave whole; peel and crush 2 garlic cloves; chop half of the dill and all of the parsley. Add everything to an iron casserole dish with $^1/_4$ cup of the good olive oil. Heat gently with the lid on for 15 minutes, until the shallots begin to soften.

2 Peel, seed and chop the tomatoes. Add them to the casserole dish. Shell the fava beans and peas and add them. Add the artichoke heart (if you are using one), plus the water, the lemon juice, and 2 teaspoons of salt. Cover and cook gently for 25 minutes. Add the asparagus (if you are using any) and cook for a final 3 minutes. Keep warm.

3 Season the turbot with salt and pepper and roll in flour. Pan fry in the $^1/_2$ cup of light olive oil, for approximately 5 minutes until the fish is firm and cooked.

4 Sear the scallops in an almost dry pan until just cooked.

5 Make up the dressing by liquidizing the remaining $\frac{1}{4}$ cup of good olive oil, the last garlic clove, the basil, and the remaining dill. Adjust seasoning with salt.

Shopping and showing off

While not ideal, this dish will work with frozen vegetables. It should be served in soup bowls; ladle in the vegetable mixture, add a crisply fried turbot fillet and dress each portion with two scallops. Drizzle a little of the dressing over the fish.

Honey and ginger roast octopus

This is a typical Livebait dish, at first glance very simple but also quite intricate; and the octopus keeps its character. Serve it with a crisp Salade Niçoise – this is one they wouldn't recognize in Nice! Serves two.

$4\frac{1}{2}$ cups water

$4\frac{1}{2}$ cups malt vinegar

3 cups cheap red wine

4 bay leaves

10 coriander seeds

10 black peppercorns

3-inch piece root ginger

$2\frac{1}{4}$ pound cleaned octopus

5 tablespoons honey

juice of 3 limes

I fat red chili pepper

3 tablespoons very finely chopped crystallized ginger

I quantity Salade Niçoise (see page 28)

1 Take a large stainless steel saucepan (aluminum or other reactive pans may leave a "taint"). Add the water, vinegar, wine, bay leaves, coriander seeds and peppercorns. Peel the root ginger and add in ¾-inch chunks.

2 Add the octopus and bring to a boil, reduce to a simmer until cooked – which is when the point of a knife slips easily into it – about an hour. Lift the octopus out and discard the liquid.

3 Preheat your oven to 400°F.

4 Dissolve the honey in the lime juice by warming them together in a stainless steel pan. Add the chili, chopped finely – discard the seeds if you do not like your dishes hot – and the crystallized ginger.

5 Cut the octopus into manageable pieces and use a pastry brush to paint them with the warm marinade.

6 Put the octopus into a roasting pan and roast in a hot oven for 15 minutes: overcooking will make the meat tough.

continued overleaf

Shopping and showing off

First choice is the kind of octopus known as a "red" octopus. These come from the Mediterranean and Aegean seas, and can be distinguished from the Atlantic octopus by the double row of suckers they have on each tentacle. Octopus can be bought at fish stores and in some supermarkets, usually frozen. For this dish frozen octopus is a perfectly good option. Once you have boiled the octopus it will keep in a refrigerator for up to 3 days before you roast it. To serve, pile the warm octopus in the middle of a plate and arrange the Salade Niçoise in a ring around it – sprinkle a little extra dressing on the salad.

Sea scallops with vegetable tagine

Time for something that is both simple and exotic. Spicy, slightly crunchy vegetables perfectly complement the sweet but firm scallop meat. Any tagine left over should be saved for bread making (see page 149). Serves two.

$\frac{1}{3}$ cup onions

2 teaspoons light olive oil

4 oz carrots

4 oz bulb fennel

4 oz parsnips

4 oz zucchini

2 teaspoons Chermoula (see page 181)

2 cups Chicken Stock (see page 188)

4 sea scallops

1 quantity Hot Chili Vinaigrette (see page 193)

1 Slice the onions and cook with the oil in a heavy saucepan until soft.

2 Peel the vegetables and cut them into batons about 1½ inches long by ½ inch square (you should have about ¾ cup of each when you are done).

3 Add the Chermoula to the pan, stir in the carrots, fennel, parsnips and zucchini and fry the mixture. As the vegetables to color, add the chicken stock.

4 Simmer for 25 minutes, or until all the stock is absorbed. Keep warm.

5 Season the scallops with sea salt and freshly ground black pepper, and sear them in a hot pan – they are done when they are firm to the touch. Try to avoid overcooking them.

Shopping and showing off

You should ask your fishmonger for the largest fresh sea scallops: he will be happy to clean them for you. If they are monsters – shells about 7 inches across – slice them in half. Frozen scallops will do, but defrost them conscientiously and pat them dry. Arrange a pile of tagine on each plate, then add two scallops, and drizzle over some Hot Chili Vinaigrette for a bit more bite.

dinners à deux

Spring rolls of squid, oyster and bacon
with chicory frisée and shiitake mushrooms,
apple and raisin chutney

These seriously tasty spring rolls come with an elegant side salad topped with the tentacles of the squid, which are broiled until crisp. While you need to be neat and methodical in your approach, no special techniques are required. Serves two.

1⅔ cups dried shiitake mushrooms

¾ pound cleaned squid including tentacles

2½ ounces smoked bacon

6 opened oysters

squeeze of lemon juice

1 bunch scallions

2 tablespoons light olive oil

½ cup crème fraîche

salt and pepper

6 sheets ready-made phyllo pastry

4 tablespoons melted butter

1 egg

1 head chicory frisée

1 quantity Balsamic Vinaigrette (see page 193)

1 quantity Apple and Raisin Chutney (see page 185)

1 Preheat your oven to 425°F.

2 Soak the mushrooms in warm water for at least an hour.

3 Cut the squid bodies into large dice (about ¾-inch square), put the tentacles aside.

4 Cut the rind from the bacon, and chop into small dice.

5 Poach the oysters until just firming up – about 1 minute in simmering water that has had a squeeze of lemon juice added – remove with a slotted spoon.

6 Chop the scallions and fry them in a little oil with the bacon. After 5 minutes, add the bits of squid body, and the mushrooms, drained and chopped coarsely. Stir and cook for a further 2 minutes.

7 Allow the mixture to cool, then add the oysters and crème fraîche. Adjust the seasoning.

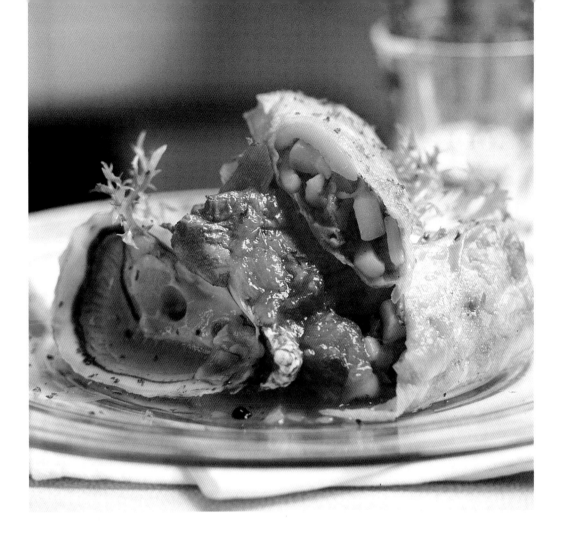

8 Lay out a sheet of phyllo, paint with melted butter, and then top with a second sheet. Cut the sheets down the middle. Each narrow strip will make a spring roll.

9 Place a dollop of mixture on the sheet and roll, turning the edges in to make a spring roll. There should be six in all.

10 Put the spring rolls on a greased baking sheet, and beat an egg. Paint the spring rolls with the egg wash and bake for 8–10 minutes.

11 Meanwhile, brush the tentacles with olive oil and cook until crisp under the broiler.

Shopping and showing off

Fishmongers in Britain tend to pander to their customers' prejudices by discarding the tentacles when selling squid. This is a shame as tentacles are wonderful when crisped up. Insist on getting yours. To serve, make a nest of the chicory leaves, fill with the three spring rolls and top with the tentacles. Drizzle all over with Balsamic Vinaigrette, and add a dollop of Apple and Raisin Chutney on the side of the plate.

Broiled salmon on an artichoke "pizza"
with tomatoes and feta cheese

This is a luxurious dish that, on inspection, proves to be surprisingly healthy. The salmon is plainly broiled, while the dough element of a real pizza has been replaced with an artichoke heart. The sauce is simply the liquid the artichoke has been cooked in. Fish, vegetables, olive oil and a little cheese – the perfect Mediterranean combination. Serves two.

2 globe artichokes

1 lemon

1 cup medium sweet white wine

6 plum tomatoes

2 cloves garlic

4 packed cups flat parsley leaves

salt and pepper

1 bunch fresh basil

2 (6-ounce) pieces of salmon fillet

2 tablespoons good olive oil

$\frac{1}{4}$ pound soft feta cheese

1 First prepare the artichokes. Take off two layers of leaves and then slice through horizontally. Trim back to reveal the hairy choke in the center and remove it with a teaspoon; be sure you leave a bowl-shaped depression in the center of each heart. Halve the lemon and rub the trimmed hearts with one half, then put them into water with the juice from the whole lemon to stop them going dark.

2 Put the white wine in a saucepan, and boil intensively to cook off the alcohol – this should take 3–4 minutes.

3 Drain the artichokes upside down on paper towels.

4 Core, skin and seed the plum tomatoes; chop them coarsely. Chop the garlic cloves and the parsley. Put it all into a heavy, lidded pan with the reduced wine and a teaspoon of salt. Stir, and sit the artichokes in the mixture. Put the lid on and cook very slowly for about 25 minutes or until the artichokes are tender.

5 Tear the basil leaves into strips, add them to the pot, and remove from the heat; check the seasoning.

6 Season the salmon, then oil and cook it under a hot broiler for 3 minutes a side, skin side first.

7 At the same time, use the other side of your broiler to finish the artichokes. Use a slotted spoon to remove them from the sauce, then pop some of the tomato pieces into the depression in the middle of each, drizzle with a little olive oil, sprinkle with the feta and broil.

8 Season the remaining juices with salt and pepper.

Shopping and showing off

Any robust white wine will do – at Livebait we use an Alsatian Riesling. To serve, simply balance the salmon on the top of the artichoke and surround with the tomatoey cooking juices.

Sea scallops with roast quince and cardoon

This dish provides an amazing combination of tastes and textures: the sweetness of the scallops, the tang of the quince and the salty crunch of the cardoon. Take heart in the face of such obscure fruit and vegetables: a pear will easily stand in for a quince, and you can substitute red Swiss chard or celery for the cardoons. If you have a helpful greengrocer, do try the dish in all its glory, you will find it well worth the effort. Serves two.

2 quinces *or* pears

$\frac{1}{2}$ cup white wine

3 tablespoons honey

I small onion

2 tablespoons olive oil

I head cardoon *or* red Swiss chard *or* celery

$2\frac{1}{4}$ cups white wine

$2\frac{1}{4}$ cups Chicken Stock (see page 188)

4 large sea scallops

juice of 2 lemons

rind of I lemon

6 ounces (I $\frac{1}{2}$ sticks) butter, cold from the refrigerator

salt

I Preheat your oven to 350°F.

2 Mix the white wine and honey. Then peel and core the quinces and paint with the mixture.

2 Roast on a tray in the oven for 2 hours – or 20–30 minutes if you are using pears. Put to the side.

3 Peel the onion and chop finely; cook with a little oil in a large saucepan until translucent.

4 Peel the cardoon or celery to remove the strings. If you're using Swiss chard, trim it carefully. Cut into I $\frac{1}{2}$-inch lengths and add to the saucepan, with the wine and chicken stock.

5 Simmer for between 60 and 80 minutes for cardoons or celery, and just 45 minutes for Swiss chard. Drain, and reserve the vegetables and the cooking liquid. All of the above may be done well in advance of finishing the dish.

6 Put the quince or pear, and the cardoon, celery or chard into a slow oven to warm through while you sear the scallops in a lightly oiled heavy pan. Do not overcook them: they are done when they are firm to the touch. Reserve, while you make the sauce.

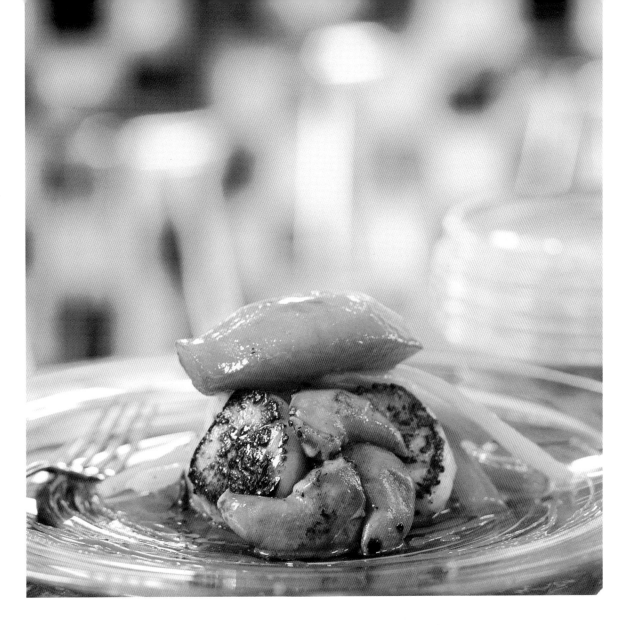

7 Put the lemon juice and rind into a pan, and heat up. Add ¼ cup of the cardoon cooking liquid. Reduce the pan juices by a third . Cut the butter into small cubes, and add them a couple at a time while whisking. The sauce should be thickened and glossy. Adjust the seasoning.

Shopping and showing off

You should ask your fishmonger for large fresh scallops – allow two per person. Frozen scallops will do, but defrost them conscientiously and pat them dry. Arrange the quince in the center of the plate, with the cardoons, chard or celery to one side. If they are very large scallops cut each one into three slices and "shingle" them. Surround with the sauce.

Lobster, Yellow Finn potato salad
with oyster mushrooms, salmon "caviar" and gazpacho sauce

Yellow Finn are the most commonly available waxy potatoes, but you can substitute another local variety. The waxiness of the potatoes teams up well with the sweetness of the lobster, and the dressing made with fresh dill is worth filing away for use with any sweet fish or shellfish. This is a dish to share, and it serves two people.

$\frac{1}{2}$ pound Yellow Finn potatoes

$\frac{1}{4}$ cup light olive oil

$\frac{1}{4}$ cup sweet sherry

$\frac{1}{3}$ cup finely chopped shallots

$\frac{2}{3}$ cup oyster mushrooms

salt and pepper

1 (2$\frac{1}{4}$-pound) cooked lobster

$\frac{1}{2}$ bunch fresh dill

2 tablespoons good olive oil

2 tablespoons sherry vinegar

2 ounces salmon "caviar"

1 quantity Gazpacho Sauce (see page 196)

1 Wash the potatoes and leave the skins on. If there are any very large ones cut them in half. Cook the potatoes in boiling water – no salt – until they are half cooked. Strain.

2 Put the olive oil into a frying pan and heat it up until smoking. Add the potatoes and stir as they seal.

3 As the potatoes cook, add the sherry and allow to reduce and caramelize.

4 Turn down the heat and cook until the potatoes are nearly done – they should have a tiny bit of "bite" to them. Stir in the raw shallots, and finally the mushrooms, which will cook very quickly.

5 Cool to lukewarm before seasoning with salt and pepper to taste.

Shopping and showing off

Supermarket lobsters are perfectly OK, but (as with all fish) fresher is always better. Best to get a live lobster and boil it yourself. If you settle for precooked lobster do not despair: they need a little "help" and this is just the recipe to make them shine. If you are the sort of person who doesn't have sweet sherry in the house, simply add 2 teaspoons of brown sugar to dry sherry. Split the lobster and take the shell off the tail section, leave the head on, and crack the claws. Snip the dill finely, and mix with the olive oil and sherry vinegar. Pour over the exposed tail meat. Serve this dish by arranging a central mound of potato salad, top it with salmon "caviar" and curl the half lobster around it. Add the dill dressing to the lobster meat, and a pool of Gazpacho Sauce on the other side of the plate.

dishes from left field

Roulade of home-cured mackerel and prosciutto, with fresh cod roe sauce *(see opposite)* 128   Panfried fish bundles with red pepper coulis 130   **Lasagne of sole and spinach in a Stilton béchamel sauce, with leaves, cornichons and capers 132**   Meatballs of whole scallops within spicy sausagemeat, coral sauce and shredded snow peas 134   **Roast gigot of monkfish and belly pork, with gigandaes plaki 136**   "Confit" of shark with celeriac remoulade 138   **Salmon with a vanilla pod sauce and foie gras ravioli 140**

Roulade of home-cured mackerel and prosciutto, with fresh cod roe sauce

This dish looks most elegant and the fresh cod roe sauce is particularly fine. Do try and get fresh cod roe: smoked cod roe will do as an alternative, but it is a great deal less subtle. Serves four.

4 fillets Home-Cured Mackerel (see page 202)

8 small slices prosciutto *or* 4 large ones

2 red onions

I cup fish stock

$\frac{2}{3}$ cup sweetish white wine

$\frac{1}{4}$ cup heavy cream

4 ounces fresh *or* smoked cod roe

salt and pepper

paprika

juice of I lemon

some salad leaves

I Scrape the cured mackerel from the skin, avoiding any dark bits. Chop it finely.

2 Lay out the prosciutto and cover it with the chopped mackerel. Then roll each slice up to make a roulade.

3 To make the sauce, first cook the onions in the stock until the liquid has reduced by two-thirds.

4 Add the wine and reduce by two-thirds.

5 Pass through a sieve (or process in a food processor). Then add the cream, and reduce by half.

6 Scrape the roe from its skin while the sauce base cools slightly (you don't want the cod eggs scrambling). Then whisk the roe into the cream mixture. Check the seasoning, which will vary wildly depending on whether you have used fresh or smoked roe, and adjust with salt, pepper, paprika and lemon juice. The sauce should be "grainy" in the mouth.

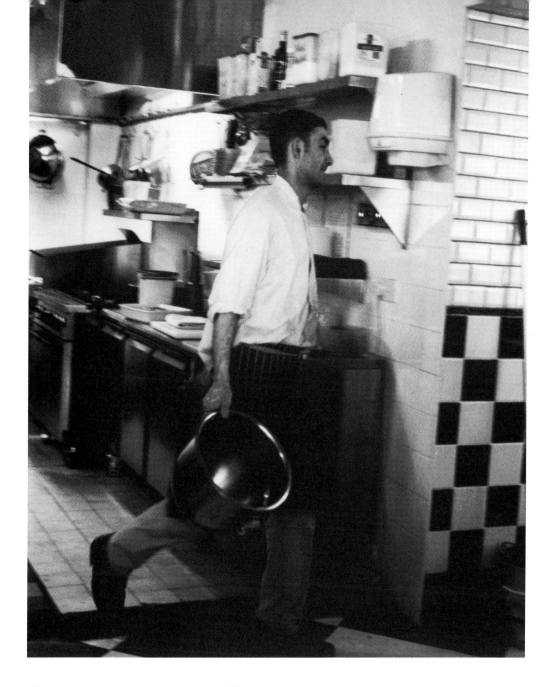

Shopping and showing off

Cut each roulade through the middle into two slices and arrange these on the plate with a puddle of sauce. Add some sharp tasting leaves – like arugula – for garnish and contrast. The fresh cod roe sauce will solidify as it cools so it needs to be warm when served. It's worth making a double quantity of this sauce if you have been lucky enough to get hold of fresh cod roe, as any surplus sauce can be used to make a delicious supper dish. Simply spread a piece of toast with the solidified sauce and pop it under the broiler for a minute.

Panfried fish bundles

with red pepper coulis

There are two ways of ensuring that these fish bundles hold together: if you have a helpful butcher, ask him to let you have some caul fat; if not, use a couple of slices of Parma ham to make neat parcels. The Red Pepper Coulis (see page 199) gives a welcome splash of color. Makes eight substantial and filling bundles – serves four.

2 red onions

1 clove garlic

2 tablespoons olive oil

1 fat red chili pepper

$^3/_4$ pound flounder

1 pound hake

2 large sea scallops

$^1/_4$ pound peeled and deveined Atlantic shrimp

2 eggs

$^1/_2$ bunch parsley

4 tablespoons white breadcrumbs

$^1/_2$ pound caul fat *or* 16 slices Parma ham

salt and pepper

1 quantity Red Pepper Coulis (see page 199)

1 Preheat your oven to 400°F.

2 Chop the onions and garlic finely and soften in 2 tablespoons of the olive oil with the chili, which should be chopped finely, and seeded if you want to moderate its heat.

3 Skin the flounder and turbot.

4 Take the scallops, shrimp, flounder and hake. Mince a third, and chop the other two thirds finely. Beat the eggs, and add them to the fish with the onion mixture, finely chopped parsley and the breadcrumbs. Mix well.

5 Check the seasoning by taking a spoonful of the mix and frying it, then taste and adjust the mixture with salt and pepper.

6 Make up patties with about 4 ounces of mixture in each. Secure with caul fat – just one layer, or the fatty taste will dominate – or make into parcels with two sheets of Parma ham per bundle.

7 Brown in a frying pan before transferring to the oven for 6–7 minutes.

dishes from left field

Shopping and showing off

Instead of flounder you can substitute other white fish. Frozen sea scallops will do nicely. To serve, float the bundles on a sea of Red Pepper Coulis.

Lasagne of sole and spinach

in a Stilton béchamel sauce, with leaves, cornichons and capers

Complex salads in which every texture and taste plays a part are a feature of many Livebait dishes. Here a spare salad partners a very strange lasagne which sheds a new light on Stilton. Serves four.

$\frac{1}{4}$ pound (1 stick) plus 2 tablespoons butter

$\frac{1}{2}$ cup flour, plus a little extra

$2\frac{1}{4}$ cups milk

1 teaspoon nutmeg

1 teaspoon paprika

$\frac{1}{4}$ pound mature Stilton cheese

$\frac{1}{2}$ pound Caerphilly cheese

14 lasagne noodles

$2\frac{1}{4}$ pounds spinach

$4\frac{1}{4}$ pounds sole fillets

paprika

salt and pepper

1 bunch flat-leafed parsley

$\frac{2}{3}$ cup cornichons

$\frac{1}{4}$ cup capers

10 scallions

1 quantity Balsamic Vinaigrette (see page 193)

1 Preheat your oven to 350°F.

2 Make a béchamel sauce by melting $\frac{1}{4}$ pound of the butter in a pan, then adding the flour and cooking it gently. (Be careful that it doesn't turn brown, merely golden.) Heat the milk to just below boiling in another saucepan and whisk it into the flour and butter a ladleful at a time. Add a little grated nutmeg and paprika.

3 Then fold in the cheeses, season to taste, and let stand.

4 Precook the lasagne noodles for 5 minutes in boiling salted water, drain and reserve.

5 Wilt the spinach in a minimum amount of boiling salted water for 1 minute and drain.

6 Skin the sole fillets, season, and sear them in a frying pan with a smear of butter.

7 Butter a 13 × 9 × 2 inch lasagne dish and you are ready to assemble. A thin layer of sauce; a layer of lasagne; a layer of sauce; a layer made with half the spinach pressed well down; a layer of lasagne; a layer of sauce; the sole fillets; a layer of lasagne; a layer of sauce; a layer made with the second half of the spinach pressed well down; a layer of lasagne; a layer of sauce.

8 Bake in the oven for 30 minutes. Then brown under the broiler if necessary.

9 Prepare the salad by chopping the flat-leafed parsley and the scallions, quartering the cornichons, and mixing them with the capers and a little Balsamic Vinaigrette (see page 193).

Shopping and showing off

If you have trouble finding flat-leafed parsley, use other salad leaves like arugula, chicory frisée or oak-leaf lettuce. The aim is a salad that provides a contrast in both tastes and textures to the rich lasagne. To serve, cut a square portion of lasagne, center it on the plate and scatter the salad around the edges.

Meatballs of whole sea scallops
within spicy sausagemeat, coral sauce and snow peas

A glass of dry cider goes well with this dish. The end result should be rather like a delicate Scotch egg but with a whole scallop as a surprise center. One makes a good starter and two a main course. The recipe serves eight.

1 red onion

$\frac{1}{2}$ bunch of parsley

1 clove garlic

2 fat red chili peppers

2 tablespoons light olive oil

1 pound pack of your favorite pork sausages

$\frac{1}{3}$ cup heavy cream

nutmeg

8 sea scallops, with their corals

2 shallots

sweet paprika

1 cup Fish Stock (see page 186)

1 cup white wine

salt and pepper

$\frac{3}{4}$ pound snow peas

2 tablespoons butter

juice of $\frac{1}{2}$ lemon

1 Preheat your oven to 400°F.

2 Chop the onion, parsley, and garlic finely; seed and chop the chilis finely. Soften everything in a frying pan with 1 tablespoon of the olive oil.

3 Rinse the sausages under the faucet, and the skins slip off easily. Amalgamate the sausagemeat with the onion mixture, add $\frac{1}{2}$ of a grated nutmeg, and 2 tablespoons of cream.

4 Strip the corals from the scallops and save them. Dry the scallops off carefully with a towel and encase each one in a layer of sausagemeat. Brown well in a frying pan to seal. You need a little practice to keep the balls shut and intact. Press the opening firmly.

5 Transfer to the oven to finish cooking for 5–7 minutes.

6 For the sauce, finely chop the shallots and soften them in the remaining 1 tablespoon of olive oil, add the corals and paprika and cook until everything is beginning to color.

continued overleaf

dishes from left field

7 Add the stock and reduce by half.

8 Add the wine and reduce by two-thirds.

9 Liquidize with a hand blender (or a food processor).

10 Thin the sauce with the remaining cream, adjust the seasoning and keep warm.

11 Top and tail the snow peas and shred them into fine strips with a sharp knife.

12 Cook them quickly in a frying pan with the lemon juice, salt, pepper and butter.

Shopping and showing off

You can use sausagemeat rather than skinning sausages, but be cautious of the seasoning as commercial sausagemeat can be very salty. To serve, use the contrasting colors of the coral sauce and the snow peas on opposite sides of the meatballs. The Red Pepper Coulis (see page 199) would make a good alternative to the coral sauce.

Roast gigot of monkfish and belly pork, with gigandaes plaki

A wild combination that is sure to surprise: firm, lean monkfish; smooth, rich belly pork; crisp, crackling, melting Greek bean dish. Try this out on the most opinionated of your foodie friends: it will impress them. But remember to start your preparations at least four days in advance so the pork can be properly brined. Serves four.

1 cup salt

1½ cups sugar

4 bay leaves

12 juniper berries

1 fat red chili pepper, finely chopped

1¾-pound-piece belly pork, from the meaty end

2 tablespoons honey

1¾-pound monkfish tail, skinned and boned

1 clove garlic

several branches of rosemary

1 tablespoon olive oil

1 quantity Gigandaes Plaki (see page 24)

1 Four days in advance, take a large crock and put in the salt, sugar, bay leaves, juniper berries and the chili. Mix well. Add 4½ cups of water and mix well to dissolve the sugar and salt. Add the pork and enough water to ensure that it is covered. Use a plate to keep the joint submerged for four days.

2 Preheat your oven to 400°F.

3 Take the pork out of the brine, and dry it with a towel. It must be very dry for good crackling. (At Livebait it gets a blast from a hairdryer to make sure!)

4 Dissolve the honey in ¼ cup of the brine liquid and paint over the skin.

5 Roast on a rack for 40 minutes. Then take out and allow to rest while you cook the monkfish.

6 Cut the garlic into slivers and tear the rosemary into sprigs. Make slits all over the monkfish and fill them alternately with garlic and rosemary. Season the fish with salt and pepper and sear it in a frying pan with a minimum of oil.

7 Put in the oven – still at 400°F – for 15–20 minutes.

Shopping and showing off

Make your butcher and fishmonger do their share. Each should be responsible for the preparation work. You need the pork closely scored and the monkfish tail boned. If the crackling doesn't come out shrapnel crisp you can finish the belly pork with a spell under the broiler while the monkfish is roasting. To serve, place a decent helping of Gigandaes Plaki in the center of a deep plate. Remove the bones from the back of the belly pork and cut the meat into generous slices. Carve similar slices off the monkfish. Arrange a slice of each on top of the plate of beans.

"Confit" of shark

with celeriac remoulade

Very few people have a good word to say about sharks – the _Jaws_ movies have a lot to answer for. In the kitchen, however, shark comes into its own – firm, solid meat that takes on other flavors well. At Livebait there is a healthy disdain for convention, and this innovative dish applies the slow cooking technique used to make duck and goose "confit" to shark . . . with fascinating results. Serves four.

1 pound 2 ounces goose fat

1 garlic clove

peel of 1 orange

6 juniper berries

12 black peppercorns

1 cinnamon stick

2 bay leaves

1 pound 2 ounces shark loin

¼ pound lean unsmoked bacon

½ cup red wine

2 tablespoons Worcestershire sauce

1 tablespoon pickled green peppercorns

1 tablespoon cold, unsalted butter

salt and pepper

1 quantity Celeriac Remoulade (see page 198)

1 Put the goose fat into a saucepan and add the garlic, finely crushed, as well as the orange peel, juniper berries, peppercorns, cinnamon and bay leaves. Heat up gently to a maximum of 130°F (you need a thermometer: if it gets too hot it will spoil). Cook for an hour.

2 Let the goose fat cool down but do not let it solidify.

3 Portion the shark into four pieces, and pierce with a small knife. Put the shark into the infused goose fat and allow to stand for at least 12 hours in a cool place.

4 Put the pan back on the heat and bring up to 140°F. Cook for 20–25 minutes.

5 To make the sauce, dice the bacon finely and fry it gently for 5–6 minutes. Turn the heat up and add the wine and Worcestershire sauce, let it bubble until reduced by half, and then whisk in the cold, cubed butter a little at a time. The sauce will thicken. Add the pickled green peppercorns at the last minute, and adjust the seasoning with salt and pepper.

Shopping and showing off

Ask your fishmonger for shark loin, including the belly. Blue shark or sand shark (dogfish) are best. If these are unavailable, substitute a piece cut from another large, firm fish such as swordfish. The most enjoyable way to secure goose fat is to tuck into a roast goose, but even the French sometimes resort to the tinned goose fat that is available from good food shops. You'll find pickled green peppercorns in small tins at smart shops. To serve, slice the shark portions, arrange them on a mound of Celeriac Remoulade and surround with the red wine sauce.

Salmon with a vanilla pod sauce
and foie gras ravioli

The very thing to bring out a flair for extravagance. If you cannot think of anywhere that might be able to get fresh foie gras for you – or merely as a stopgap during the long years when you are saving up to purchase a piece – you can make these ravioli using tinned *bloc de foie gras*. There's no denying it, fresh foie gras is much nicer.

2 large fat red chili peppers

2 mild onions

$\frac{2}{3}$ cup Sauternes *or* another sweet white wine

4 ounces fresh foie gras *or* tinned *bloc de foie gras*

1 cup chopped leeks

1 cup chopped carrots

1 cup chopped celery (preferably the leafy parts)

$1\frac{1}{2}$ cups white wine

8 black peppercorns

1 bay leaf

juice of 1 lemon

4 thick ($\frac{1}{2}$-pound) steaks cut from a large salmon

1 quantity Simple Pasta Dough (see page 200)

salt and pepper

1 quantity Vanilla Pod Sauce (see pages 196–7)

1 Roast the chilis under the broiler. Set aside in a sealed plastic bag to cool, then rub off the skins, split, and remove the seeds. Chop very finely.

2 Peel and chop the onions very finely.

3 Mix the sweet wine, chilis and chopped onions. Put the foie gras on to a plate and coat thoroughly with the mixture, cover with plastic wrap and marinate in a refrigerator for at least 12 hours.

4 Chop the leeks, carrots and celery, and add them to the wine, peppercorns, bay leaf and lemon juice in a large pan. Heat until the liquid boils; after 10 minutes turn down to a simmer and lower in the salmon steaks. Poach for 3–5 minutes – they are done if they are resilient when pressed. Skin and put to one side while you cook the ravioli.

5 Divide the pasta dough into four. Then roll it as thinly as you can. Put a quarter of the marinated foie gras and a little of the marinade in a pile, centrally on one half. Season well. Fold the other half of the sheet over. Cut out a circular ravioli about 4 inches across with the foie gras centered. Crimp the edges together with a little water.

5 Poach the ravioli in a large pan of salted water that has been brought to a rolling boil. They should take 3–4 minutes. Do them singly or in pairs – they should never be crowded.

Shopping and showing off

If you can buy ready-made fresh ravioli dough, well and good. To serve, cover the salmon with a good layer of Vanilla Pod Sauce or, if you prefer, use the Sauce Choron (see page 195). Add a ravioli to the side of each piece of salmon and pour a little sauce over the fish.

bread

At Livebait we worry about the bread. It may have a strictly supporting role, but if something goes wrong with the day's baking there is no way of getting things back to an even keel. Customers will be grumpy. The chefs will be at odds with the wait staff. It guarantees discontent. On the other hand, when crisp-crusted loaves of brightly colored, delicious-smelling breads are circulating around the dining room, you can hear the admiring murmurs, all is right with the world, and the service will go by in a flash.

Yeast is the magic ingredient, both in the making of bread and the brewing of bread's cousin, alcohol. Who would have thought that a talent for breathing out CO_2 and the consequent by-products would prove so useful? Bread is made from flour, water, yeast and a little salt, yet as with every superficially simple recipe, once you have grasped the ingredients list your troubles have only just begun. Weighty volumes have been written about bread-making and its mysteries, but few authors have isolated the two key factors.

1 Practice: bread-making is something you teach yourself. If you made a couple of loaves of bread every day, pretty soon you would become good at it. What's more, all the minor adjustments, do's, don'ts and precautions that take up so much room in the books would soon become second nature. With practice, bread-making is much easier than you think. Persevere. At Livebait we get the constant practice we need.

2 Flexibility: weights, measures, timings, oven heats and so forth are not carved in stone. If you use only a very little yeast to make dough, and then leave it to rise in a cool place, the process may take a lot longer but it will still rise in the end. Similarly, warm the ingredients and everything will happen more quickly. Be flexible about things: there are bound to be some days when you have more time to play with than others; adapt your method to suit. Try things out.

Getting started

A bit of wise shopping can make the whole bread-making process easier.

Flour: at Livebait we use strong, white, organic flour. "Strong" refers to the amount of gluten in the flour. Strong flours are made from hard grain, which is usually grown in a cold climate. The crusty outside of a French baguette often owes its charm to strong Canadian wheat. We use white flour because we make a lot of colored breads and they look brighter. We use organic flour from a small supplier because the larger millers use steel roller mills that work much faster than traditional millstones but also generate a lot of heat – heat that can "cook" the flour a little even before it gets into the bag.

Yeast: live baker's yeast. Thank goodness that some of the large supermarket chains are so keen to convince us of the authenticity of their bakery operations that they will give away fresh yeast to anyone who asks politely! Otherwise it can be bought from some bakers and supermarkets. Dried yeast is second best, and if circumstances force you into using it, follow the directions on the packet.

Salt: we use sea salt at Livebait, both within the dough and as a topping. Minute amounts of trace elements make sea salt taste better, and nothing beats it for crunch when sprinkled on a crusty loaf.

Understanding the chemistry

Yeast loves warm, wet and sweet; but is not so keen on the cold or salt! The flour needs physical pummeling to activate the gluten and form a loaf with a good strong structure – the higher the gluten in the flour to begin with the less kneading you have to do.

So all bread-making, however fancy, comes down to a seven-stage plan:

1 Mixing flour, water, salt and yeast thoroughly.
2 Kneading the gluten.
3 Leaving the dough for the yeast to work and the bread to rise.
4 Knocking back the dough once again, to break up the bubbles made by the yeast and distribute them evenly.
5 Leaving the loaves to rise a second time.
6 Baking.
7 Cooling.

Grasp that and you're ready to bake.

bread

Basic white bread with poppy seeds

At Livebait we always keep back some dough from the previous day to mix with the new batch. This old dough, which has spent the night (or even two or three days – keep it until it smells unreasonably sour) in the refrigerator rising slowly, helps give our bread real character. But, obviously, the first time you bake you do not have any aged dough on hand, so this initial recipe uses just flour. On subsequent baking days replace about 10 percent by weight of the flour with dough. As we are baking in batches we use a large mixer with a dough hook to knead; thankfully, at home you do not have to forgo the pleasure of kneading by hand. A large-bowl food processor, however, works perfectly well.

1 tablespoon yeast

1 teaspoon sugar

2½ cups lukewarm water

7½ cups flour

1 tablespoon salt

1 egg

2 teaspoons poppy seeds

butter to grease the baking sheet

1 Dissolve the yeast with the sugar in a little of the water, and wait until it is frothy.

2 Mix the flour and salt on a work surface.

3 Make a well in the center of the heap. Add the rest of the water to the yeast mixture. Draw the flour together by pouring the liquid into the middle, and making a dough by hand.

4 Knead. Remember, you are "stretching" the gluten within the flour, and that is what you should do with the dough. After 7–8 minutes the feel of the dough will change: in some magical way it stops feeling sticky. Whether you are working by hand or with a machine, the dough is ready when you spread a little out between your hands and it stretches to a very thin skin without breaking.

5 Oil a bowl and put the dough into it. Cover it with a cloth and let it rise for hour or two; in the refrigerator it may take a day or two.

6 When the dough has doubled in size, return it to the work surface and knead until you have knocked the puffiness out of it.

7 Form it into two long, oval loaves. Put them on a greased baking sheet and set aside to rise for 45 minutes.

8 Preheat your oven to 450°F.

9 When they have risen, paint the tops of the loaves with egg wash (an egg lightly beaten with 1 teaspoon of water) and sprinkle with poppy seeds. Then make a series of knife cuts across each loaf, on the diagonal and about ¾ inch deep.

10 Bake in the oven for 35–40 minutes. Bread is cooked when you can tap the bottom with your finger and it sounds hollow. There is no substitute for experience in judging this; the sooner you start baking regularly the sooner you'll be doing it confidently.

11 When it is cooked, cool on a rack before slicing. Warm bread is delicious, but hot bread is horrid – there has not been a chance for the structure inside to firm up, or for a crust to harden.

bread

147

Strange breads

When Yannick Tual joined the kitchen at Livebait Covent Garden, he came with a sheaf of French college qualifications. A four-year course in advanced bread-making was one of them, and when he first arrived he was able to state categorically that the fancy breads we serve would be quite impossible to make: the recipes would never work – the resulting loaves would be disastrous. After seeing these brightly colored, strangely flavored crusty loaves wolfed down by a steady stream of delighted diners, he has come round to our way of thinking.

The key to inventing new breads is to liquidize whatever you wish to add, then treat the liquid as part of the water content of the dough. Obviously, this strategy works better in some cases than in others but, as with everything to do with bread, experiment until you feel it is working well, then make a note of the particular details for future reference. For the exotic combinations that follow, use the basic bread recipe and adjust as indicated. As you will probably be trying these recipes when you have already made some bread, they include some "old dough," which should be worked into the new batch with everything else. If you have no old dough simply add another ¾ cup flour.

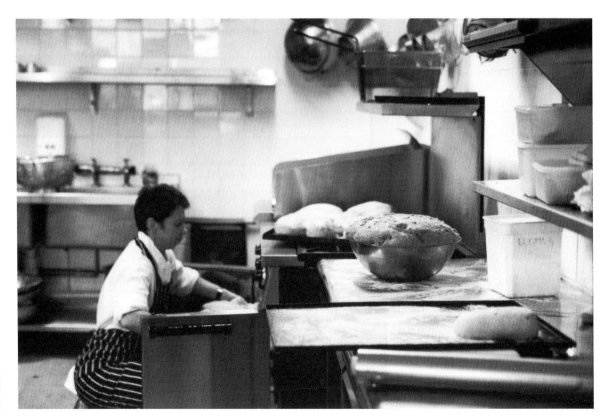

Yellow bread – tagine and turmeric

1 tablespoon yeast

1 teaspoon sugar

1 cup minus 3 tablespoons water

1¾ cups liquidized Vegetable Tagine (see page 117)

7 cups flour

1 tablespoon ground turmeric

1 tablespoon salt

¾ cup yesterday's dough

1 egg for egg wash

butter to grease the baking sheet

Red bread – Chili Jam and paprika

1 tablespoon yeast

1 teaspoon sugar

1¾ cups water

1 cup minus 3 tablespoons Chili Jam (see page 182)

7 cups flour

1 tablespoon sweet paprika

1 tablespoon salt

¾ cup yesterday's dough

1 egg for egg wash

butter to grease the baking sheet

Green bread – spinach and raisins

1 tablespoon yeast

1 teaspoon sugar

1 $\frac{3}{4}$ cups water

$\frac{1}{2}$ cup liquidized frozen spinach

7 cups flour

3 tablespoons raisins

1 tablespoon salt

$\frac{3}{4}$ cup yesterday's dough

1 egg for egg wash

butter to grease the baking sheet

Baba ganoush and lemon zest bread

1 tablespoon yeast

1 teaspoon sugar

1 $\frac{3}{4}$ cups water

1 cup minus 3 tablespoons Baba Ganoush (see page 198)

7 cups flour

zest of 1 lemon

1 tablespoon salt

$\frac{3}{4}$ cup yesterday's dough

1 egg for egg wash

butter to grease the baking sheet

Coconut and ginger bread

1 tablespoon yeast

1 teaspoon sugar

3 cups minus 3 tablespoons water

1½ cups grated coconut

7 cups flour

3 tablespoons root ginger, chopped finely

1 tablespoon salt

¾ cup yesterday's dough

1 egg for egg wash

butter to grease the baking sheet

Onion and thyme bread

1 tablespoon yeast

1 teaspoon sugar

1¾ cups water

¾ cup Red Onion Jam (see page 182)

7 cups flour

1 bunch fresh thyme, finely chopped

1 tablespoon salt

¾ cup yesterday's dough

1 egg for egg wash

butter to grease the baking sheet

Sun-dried tomato and mozzarella bread

1 tablespoon yeast

1 teaspoon sugar

2 cups water

1 1/2 cups drained and finely chopped sun-dried tomatoes

7 cups flour

4 ounces mozzarella, finely diced

1 tablespoon salt

3/4 cup yesterday's dough

1 egg for egg wash

butter to grease the baking sheet

Mussel and fennel seed bread

1 tablespoon yeast

1 teaspoon sugar

2 1/2 cups water

1 cup cooked mussels

7 cups flour

1 tablespoon fennel seeds

1 tablespoon salt

3/4 cup yesterday's dough

1 egg for egg wash

butter to grease the baking sheet

bread

153

Fennel and saffron bread

1 tablespoon yeast

1 teaspoon sugar

2 cups water

$^1/_2$ pound bulb fennel (braised in 1 cup of white wine with $^1/_2$ teaspoon saffron, then liquidized)

7 cups flour

1 tablespoon salt

$^3/_4$ cup yesterday's dough

1 egg for egg wash

butter to grease the baking sheet

Salt cod and black olive bread

1 tablespoon yeast

1 teaspoon sugar

$2^1/_4$ cups water

1 scant cup liquidized Brandade Mashed
Potatoes (see page 26)

7 cups flour

$^1/_2$ cup halved, stoned black olives

$1^1/_2$ teaspoons salt

$^3/_4$ cup yesterday's dough

1 egg for egg wash

butter to grease the baking sheet

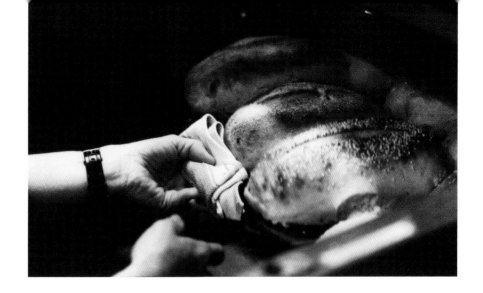

Smoked salmon and green peppercorn bread

1 tablespoon yeast

1 teaspoon sugar

2$\frac{1}{2}$ cups water

4 ounces smoked salmon cut into long thin strips

7 cups flour

2 tablespoons pickled green peppercorns

1$\frac{1}{2}$ teaspoons salt

$\frac{3}{4}$ cup yesterday's dough

1 egg for egg wash

butter to grease the baking sheet

Potato bread

1 tablespoon yeast

1 teaspoon sugar

2 cups lukewarm water

3$\frac{1}{4}$ cups flour

2$\frac{1}{2}$ cups plain, well-mashed potato

1 tablespoon salt

1 egg for egg wash

butter to grease the baking sheet

Brioche

This is it then, the ultimate challenge. Very rich, very extravagant, and seriously delicious. There is speculation that when Marie Antoinette said, "If the poor have no bread, then let them eat cake," brioche is what she had in mind. Brioche certainly *is* a bread, but only just!

1 ½ teaspoons yeast

3 tablespoons warm milk

1 teaspoon salt

2 ½ cups flour

6 eggs

6 ounces (1 ½ sticks) unsalted butter

3 scant tablespoon superfine sugar

1 Use a food mixer: it will shorten the procedure. Start by beating the yeast and the warm milk slowly with a wire whisk until frothy. Add the salt.

2 Change to a dough hook and, at a slow speed, add the flour and 5 of the eggs.

3 Melt the butter and stir the sugar into it.

4 Add the butter mixture a little at a time with the machine running; you should be sure that each dose of mixture is absorbed before adding the next.

5 After about 10 minutes, the mixture should be shiny, elastic and glossy.

6 Transfer to an oiled bowl, cover with a cloth and put in a warm place to rise.

7 When the dough has doubled in size – 1 or 2 hours, depending on how warm its resting place – remove it from the bowl and flip it lightly with your fingers to "knock it back."

8 Return it to the bowl and put it into the refrigerator for several hours to rest (but no longer than 24 hours).

9 A saucepan with an ovenproof handle makes a fine stand-in brioche mold, so take one that's about 8 inches in diameter and line it with a large sheet of greased baking parchment, being sure that it comes up above the rim. Work your dough into a suitably sized ball and put it into the saucepan.

10 Take the remaining egg and paint the top of the brioche with its yolk. Don't let the glaze run into any cracks in the dough, or "glue" the sides of the brioche to the pan or paper, as this will inhibit the final rising. Put the pan in a warm place while the brioche rises. Once again it will nearly double its bulk. To bake, preheat your oven to 450°F.

11 Bake for 40–45 minutes.

12 When cooked, remove from the saucepan and cool on a wire rack.

sweets

Chocolate and orange cake

with vanilla sauce

This is a chocolate layer cake which at Livebait is made using a large patisserie ring. In the home kitchen it is easier to assemble it in a deep-sided 8-inch cake pan. This cake will make six good slices.

6 eggs, separated

$1\frac{2}{3}$ cups superfine sugar

$\frac{1}{2}$ cup cornflour

$\frac{1}{2}$ cup flour

$\frac{2}{3}$ cup cocoa

$\frac{1}{2}$ cup heavy cream

$\frac{1}{2}$ cup milk

1 cup freshly squeezed orange juice

3 tablespoons glucose

27 squares dark baking chocolate

1 quantity Vanilla Sauce (see page 177)

1 Preheat your oven to 425°F.

2 Whisk the egg yolks with 6 tablespoons of the sugar until the mixture is fluffy and looks "white."

3 In another bowl whisk the egg whites, gradually add 2 tablespoons of sugar, and whisk until they hold a firm peak.

4 Put the cornflour, flour and 5 teaspoons of the cocoa into a sieve and work them gradually into the egg yolk mixture.

5 Fold the combination of flour, sugar and yolks into the egg whites.

6 Divide the mixture into three and cook in 8-inch cake pans. Spread the mixture out with a spatula.

7 Bake for 15–20 minutes. Remove from the oven and put flat on a work surface to cool.

8 To make the cocoa syrup, dissolve the remaining sugar in $\frac{1}{2}$ cup water and add 5 teaspoons of the cocoa. Stir to mix thoroughly and cool.

9 To make the orange chocolate ganache, bring the cream, milk, orange juice and glucose to a boil, and take off the heat.

10 Melt the chocolate in a double boiler, then steadily whisk the hot orange cream into the chocolate.

11 To assemble the cake, take an 8-inch spring-sided cake pan and use it as a mold for the three discs of cake. Place the first one in the bottom of the pan and brush liberally with the cocoa syrup.

12 To make the next layer, use half the orange chocolate ganache, evenly spread with a spatula.

13 Then another layer of cake brushed with syrup.

14 Then the rest of the ganache.

15 Brush the underside of the last piece of cake with syrup and add it.

16 Put the cake into the refrigerator for 30 minutes to set.

Shopping and showing off

If you cannot obtain glucose, use a similar weight of sugar. To serve, sift a little cocoa powder onto the top of the cake before slicing; surround each slice with Vanilla Sauce.

Almond Pithiviers

with bitter chocolate sauce

The best Pithiviers are made from a tightly layered butter puff pastry. One of the patissiers at Livebait, Yannick Tual, used to work for Monsieur Gouin Régis of Mortagne au Perche, the same Monsieur Gouin Régis who regularly won the annual Pithiviers competition held in the town of that name. The Livebait Pithiviers is the real thing – melting pastry and with a rich heart. If you would rather substitute bought ready-made puff pastry, it will still be delicious, but Gouin Régis would certainly raise an eyebrow. Makes a Pithiviers about 9 inches in diameter. Serves eight.

3 cups flour

1 teaspoon salt

1 pound (4 sticks) butter

8 tablespoons water

3 eggs

1 cup superfine sugar

1 cup ground almonds

1 quantity Bitter Chocolate Sauce (see page 177)

1 Take 2 cups of flour, and the salt. Rub in 2 tablespoons of the butter with your fingertips. Make it into pastry with the water. Cover it with plastic wrap and rest it in the refrigerator for 2–3 hours.

2 Take half (2 sticks) of the butter – cold from the refrigerator. Place it on a board and hit it with your rolling pin until it is malleable but still cold and firm. Level it out so that you have a flat piece of butter.

3 Flour the work surface and roll out the pastry into a rough square. Then roll each side until it makes a broad cross. Put the cold butter into the center of the cross and fold in the arms to enclose the butter. Put the whole thing back in the refrigerator for 30 minutes.

4 Put the pastry onto a floured work surface with the "joins" underneath and gently roll it out into a rectangle three times as long as it is wide, and about $\frac{1}{8}$-inch thick.

5 Fold the left third into the middle, and do the same with the right third. Take the square you now have and roll it out into a rectangle once more, working away from you.

6 When you have a rectangle again, fold each half in as before to make a square. Scratch an arrow on it lightly to show the direction of the last rolling. Wrap it up and rest it in the refrigerator.

sweets

continued overleaf

7 Repeat steps 5 and 6, rolling it out at right angles to the previous direction.

8 Again: repeat steps 5 and 6, rolling it out at right angles to the previous direction. Congratulations, you have butter puff pastry!

9 Preheat your oven to 400°F.

10 Beat the eggs in a bowl.

11 Make the almond filling by creaming together the remaining $\frac{1}{2}$ pound (2 sticks) of butter and 1 cup of sugar; work in the ground almonds and half the eggs. Reserve the other half of the eggs for egg wash.

12 Take half the pastry and roll it out. Use a suitable saucepan lid to mark out a circle about 9 inches in diameter.

13 Spread the filling carefully in the center of the circle. It should be $\frac{3}{8}$-inch thick and there should be a 1-inch border all the way around the edge.

14 Roll out the other half of the pastry as a lid and press the border down hard. You should end up with something that looks very much like a flattened cardinal's hat.

15 Put the Pithiviers onto a parchment-lined baking sheet; make a central steam vent. Transfer to the refrigerator for at least an hour.

16 Before baking, brush with the remaining egg. Then decorate (see the photographs opposite).

17 Bake for about 30 minutes, then lift an edge carefully from the paper with a spatula; the Pithiviers is done if it is nicely browned and crisp.

Shopping and showing off

This is a difficult dish so ready-made pastry is fair enough, but not so delicious. You can make it the day before and leave it in the refrigerator overnight for its final "rest" before baking. Serve with a fanfare of boastful trumpets and some of the excellent (and very easy) Bitter Chocolate Sauce.

Lime mousse and craquelin

The craquelin makes this a very pretty dish. Like a sugary biscuit, but thin and elegant, at Livebait the craquelin is used to provide the sail for a raft of mousse. Makes a big bowl of mousse; serves at least eight.

zest of 10 limes

4 leaves gelatin *or* 2 (¼-ounce) packets gelatin powder

juice of 10 limes

pulp of 3 limes

3 cups superfine sugar

4 cups heavy cream

1 tablespoon flour

¼ pound (1 stick) butter

1 cup sliced almonds

1 Put the lime zest into cold water and bring to a boil. Sieve the zest and repeat three times. This will remove any bitterness from the lime peel.

2 Soften the gelatin sheets in a little lime juice.

3 Warm half the remaining lime juice, half the zest, and the pulp in a saucepan with 1 cup of the sugar, stirring until it is dissolved.

4 Add the softened gelatin and stir until dissolved. Allow to cool.

5 Whip the cream until it is stiff, then fold in the lime juice mixture.

6 Transfer to a bowl and allow to set in the refrigerator overnight.

7 To make the craquelin, preheat your oven to 400°F.

8 Sift together the flour and the remaining 2 cups of sugar.

9 Melt the butter and add it, with the remaining lime juice and zest, to the flour and sugar. Chop the almonds finely, then add them. Mix with your fingers until you have a gritty texture like coarse, wet sand.

10 Line a baking sheet with baking parchment. Make small piles of the craquelin mixture – about the size of a walnut. They must be well spaced as they will melt in the oven's heat and spread out like biscuits.

11 Bake for 5–7 minutes. They are cooked when they are transparent in the middle and dark around the edges.

12 When they are done, remove the tray from the oven and lift off the paper with the craquelin on it, putting it directly onto a work surface to cool quickly.

Nougat glacé Créole

This is an extremely delicious dessert that neatly balances textures and tastes. Prepare it in advance, then simply slice and serve. The only special equipment you will need is a thermometer – getting the temperature right is the key to ending up with the right texture – so it's time to retrieve that jam thermometer languishing at the back of your cupboard and put it to work. Makes about two quarts.

$^3/_4$ cup currants

$^1/_4$ cup dark rum

$^3/_4$ cup superfine sugar

$^1/_2$ cup sliced almonds

3 egg whites

$^1/_2$ cup honey

2 cups heavy cream

seasonal fruit for coulis

1 At least 24 hours before you start cooking, put the currants to soak in the rum.

2 You also need to pre-prepare the nougatine. Take $^1/_2$ cup of the sugar, put it in a dry pan. Heat it until it melts, and then continue just until it is a nice golden brown. Watch it closely or it will turn black and bitter in what seems like the twinkling of an eye.

3 Stir the sliced almonds into the liquid sugar and pour onto a baking sheet lined with baking parchment. Allow to cool. When completely cold, break into small pieces with a rolling pin, or use a food processor – you are aiming for small chunks, not dust!

4 Put the egg whites into your food processor or blender, but do not start it yet.

5 Put the honey, the remaining sugar and $^1/_4$ cup of water into a pan and boil until the temperature reaches 233°F. Use your jam thermometer and try to be precise. When the syrup reaches that temperature, turn the heat down very low.

6 Start your food processor and process until the egg whites form soft peaks. Turn it off.

7 Back to the stove: turn the heat up and wait until your thermometer reads 250°F. You must not allow your syrup to get hotter than this or it will burn.

8 Turn the food processor back on. Gradually pour the hot syrup onto the beaten egg whites while the processor is running. The two should mix together and produce a glossy Italian meringue mixture that is just as stiff as the egg whites were before you added the syrup. Turn into a large bowl and allow to cool.

9 Whip the cream until stiff – it should just form a peak.

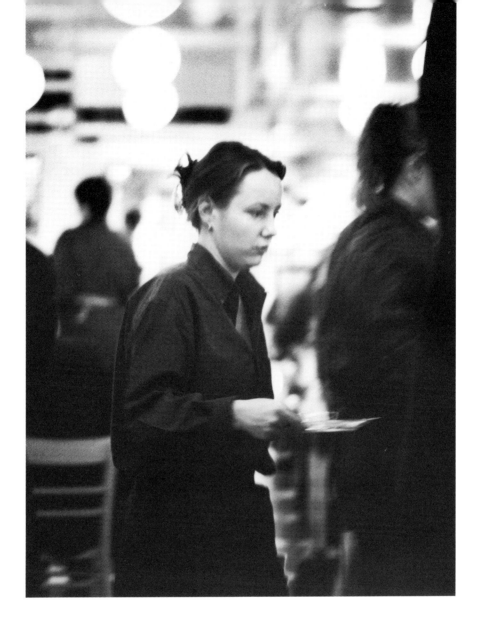

10 Fold the cream, the currants, and the nougatine into the meringue.

11 Put all the mix into a large terrine dish, or a plastic container, cover, and leave in the freezer for at least 12 hours.

Shopping and showing off

The Nougat Glacé Créole is "soft scoop" and can be served straight from the freezer. Cut slices with a serrated knife that has been dipped in hot water. To dress the plate, make a simple coulis from seasonal fruits – anything with enough acidity to give sharpness. Take half a pound of fruit and purée in a food processor, sieve to remove any seeds, and adjust the taste to suit with sugar and lemon juice.

sweets

Banana tart with lemon granita

The slight crunch of the lemon granita goes terribly well with the richness of the banana tart. At Livebait, individual tarts are the rule, but there's no reason why you shouldn't make a single large one. This recipe makes a 9-inch tart and 4 cups of granita. Serves six to eight.

zest of 8 lemons

$\frac{2}{3}$ cup lemon juice

$1\frac{2}{3}$ cups water

$\frac{2}{3}$ cup sugar

$\frac{1}{4}$ cup glucose

14 tablespoons ($1\frac{3}{4}$ sticks) butter

$\frac{3}{4}$ cup superfine sugar

1 egg

$2\frac{1}{2}$ cups flour

6 ripe bananas

1 cup ground almonds

2 egg yolks

1 First make the lemon granita. Put the lemon zest into cold water and bring to a boil. Strain the zest and repeat three times. This will remove any bitterness from the peel.

2 Warm the water, lemon juice, water, sugar and glucose in a pan. If you cannot get glucose, use $\frac{1}{2}$ cup more sugar.

3 When all is dissolved, stir in the lemon zest, pour into a plastic container, and place in the coldest part of your freezer.

4 Remove after 60 minutes and stir vigorously with a fork to break up any crystals. Put back in the freezer.

5 Repeat after another 30 minutes.

6 And once more, after another 30 minutes.

7 When you want to serve the granita, simply move it from the freezer to the refrigerator 30 minutes before you want it, and stir well before serving. It should have a slushy texture.

For the tart

1 Beat 6 tablespoons of the butter and 4 tablespoons of the sugar together in a bowl.

2 Beat the egg and work it in with a fork (saving a tiny amount to use as egg wash later).

3 Add $2\frac{1}{2}$ cups of the flour and pull together into pastry initially with a fork and then with your hands. Keep everything cool and light! Wrap the pastry in plastic wrap and put into the refrigerator to rest for at least 60 minutes.

4 Preheat your oven to 400°F.

5 Roll out the pastry until it is $\frac{1}{8}$-inch thick. Line an 8-inch tart pan or 6 individual tart cases.

6 Bake blind (put some parchment and a layer of dried beans in the tart to keep the pastry flat) for 10 minutes.

7 Remove the beans and brush the inside of the tart with a little egg wash and return to the oven for a further 3 minutes.

8 Cut the bananas into $\frac{1}{2}$-inch slices and arrange them ends down, so that they fill the pastry case.

9 Turn the oven down to 350°F and bake the tart until the banana is cooked – about 10 minutes.

10 Make the sablé topping. Use your fingertips to rub together the butter, sugar, ground almonds, and egg yolks. The mixture should end up "gritty" and feel a bit like damp sand.

11 Sprinkle the topping over the tarts until the bananas are completely covered and you have a nice flat surface. Turn the oven up to 400°F, and bake until golden brown – about 10 minutes.

Shopping and showing off

If there is no glucose at the supermarket, you can usually find it at a drugstore. Serve the tart with the granita served separately in a ramekin.

Chestnut and whiskey mousse cake

Making it into a mousse goes some way towards taming the incredible richness of chestnut purée. At Livebait we make individual mousses, but in the home it's easier to make a single cake. Use an 8-inch diameter, high-sided cake pan and you will have enough for eight slices.

5 eggs

1 1/3 cups superfine sugar

9 tablespoons (1 stick plus 1 tablespoon) melted butter

3/4 cup plus 2 tablespoons flour

1/2 cup water

9 ounces canned "crème de marrons" (sweet)

9 ounces canned "chestnut purée" (unsweetened)

5 gelatin leaves or 2 (1/4-ounce) packets gelatin powder

2 cups heavy cream

generous 1/3 cup whiskey

2 tablespoons cocoa powder

1 Preheat your oven to 425°F.

2 Whisk the eggs very well with $\frac{2}{3}$ cup of the sugar – until the mix sticks to the end of your finger. Drizzle in the melted butter and continue to beat.

3 Sift the flour slowly into the egg mixture, mixing as you go. You should end up with a mixture that resembles a very liquid mousse.

4 Line a baking sheet with baking parchment and use a spatula to spread the mixture out into a layer about $\frac{1}{2}$ inch thick.

5 Bake in the oven until golden brown – 8–10 minutes. Remove and lift the parchment and cake off the baking tray, put it down on a cold work surface to cool. This will help stop it drying out.

6 Line an 8-inch diameter high-sided cake pan with a tall funnel of baking parchment.

7 Mix the two chestnut purées together very well in a large bowl.

8 Soften the gelatin sheets (if you are not using powdered gelatin) in a little water.

9 Bring $\frac{1}{4}$ cup of the heavy cream to a boil, remove from the heat and stir in the softened gelatin sheets (or the powdered gelatin). Add $\frac{1}{2}$ cup of the whiskey and mix into the chestnut purée.

10 Whip the remaining cream until it forms soft peaks.

11 Fold it into the chestnut mixture a little at a time.

12 Warm the remaining whiskey and sugar until you have a syrup.

13 Cut a circle of cake that fits exactly and put it into the lined pan. Brush with the whiskey syrup.

14 Fill up with the chestnut mousse, banging the pan down gently to settle the mixture and drive out air pockets. Put into the refrigerator until set – about 12 hours.

15 To serve, remove from the pan, dust the top of the cake with a little cocoa, and slice.

Shopping and showing off

You may have to shop around for these chestnut products – look out for the name Clément Faugier. The crème de marrons is very sweet, the purée less so. If you can only obtain the purée, use it as a substitute for the crème and add 2 tablespoons of sugar and a few drops of vanilla essence. This dessert needs nothing added beyond a little heavy cream.

Chocolate and pear tart

You can just as easily make individual portions of this very rich tart as one large one. And if you feel an extravagant impulse coming on, you can flambé the pears in a glass of brandy rather than poach them in syrup – bearing in mind that if you choose this route you should buy slightly riper fruit. Makes a 9-inch diameter tart. Serves six.

12 tablespoons ($1\frac{1}{2}$ sticks) butter

$1\frac{1}{2}$ cups superfine sugar

1 egg

$2\frac{1}{4}$ cups flour

$1\frac{1}{2}$ cups water

1 vanilla pod

4 pears

1 cup heavy cream

$1\frac{1}{2}$ cups honey

9 (1-ounce) squares dark baking chocolate

$4\frac{1}{2}$ (1-ounce) squares sweetened baking chocolate

1 Beat the butter and $\frac{3}{4}$ cup of the sugar together in a bowl.

2 Work in the egg with a fork (saving a tiny amount to use as egg wash later).

3 Add the flour and pull together into pastry with a fork and then your hands. Keep everything cool and light! Wrap the pastry in plastic wrap and put into the refrigerator to rest for at least an hour. Take out and bring back to room temperature before rolling.

4 Preheat your oven to 400°F.

5 Roll out the pastry until it is $\frac{1}{8}$-inch thick. Use it to line a 9-inch tart pan.

6 Bake blind (put some baking parchment and a layer of dried beans in the tart to keep the pastry flat) for 20 minutes.

7 Remove the beans and brush the inside of the tart with a little egg wash and return to the oven for a further 5 minutes.

8 Meanwhile, make up a syrup by dissolving $\frac{3}{4}$ cup of sugar in $1\frac{1}{2}$ cups of water and adding a vanilla pod split lengthwise.

9 Peel, halve and core the pears and cook them in the syrup until soft. Drain and slice into pieces less than $\frac{3}{8}$-inch thick.

10 Bring the cream and honey to a boil. Remove from the heat.

11 Melt the two chocolates in a double boiler, then add them to the hot cream and honey. Stir the mixture thoroughly.

12 Arrange the pear slices in the tart case, pour over the chocolate until the pears are completely submerged and you have a smooth surface. Cool until set.

Shopping and showing off

Serve this tart alone in all its glory as it is extremely rich – the possible exception being to consider adding a dollop of clotted cream, garnished with a sprig of mint, on the edge of the plate.

Bitter chocolate sauce

So easy. So good ! Makes about two cups.

1 cup milk

6 (1-ounce) squares unsweetened baking chocolate

$\frac{1}{3}$ cup heavy cream

$3\frac{1}{2}$ tablespoons unsalted butter

1 Heat the milk until boiling in a saucepan.

2 Whisk in the chocolate, then the cream, then the butter.

Sweet vanilla sauce

This is a sophisticated kind of custard, but custard nevertheless! Makes almost four cups.

2 cups milk

2 vanilla pods

6 egg yolks

1 cup sugar

$\frac{1}{2}$ cup heavy cream

1 Put the milk into a saucepan. Split the vanilla pods lengthwise and strip the seeds into the milk, then add the pods. Bring to a boil and turn off immediately.

2 Whisk the egg yolks and sugar until they are fluffy and look "white."

3 Whip the cream.

4 Remove the vanilla pods from the milk with a straining spoon.

5 Put the egg yolk mixture into a saucepan and, over a minimal heat, steadily whisk in the hot milk. As the sauce starts to thicken, remove the pan from the heat and whisk in the whipped cream.

Shopping and Showing off

This sauce should be light and frothy and benefits from being served no hotter than lukewarm.

pickles, preserves and sauces

Tomato chutney

This is a stunning red chutney, which needs to be made from really ripe tomatoes. As tomatoes are so often only half-ripe when you buy them, remember to get them a few days in advance and allow them to ripen fully before you start. Makes about 3¼ pounds of chutney.

4-inch piece of root ginger

1 pound cooking apples

10 ounces Spanish onions

3¼ pounds ripe tomatoes

1½ cups raisins

1 cup plus 2 tablespoons dark brown sugar

2 teaspoons salt

2 cups malt vinegar

1 teaspoon cayenne pepper

2 teaspoons mustard powder

1 Peel the root ginger, cut it into 1¼-inch pieces, and bruise them with a hammer. Then tie them up in a piece of cheesecloth.

2 Peel, core and chop the apples very finely. Skin and chop the onions very finely. Skin the tomatoes and chop them coarsely.

3 Put all the ingredients and the muslin-wrapped ginger into a large nonreactive saucepan. Bring to a boil, then reduce the heat and simmer gently, uncovered, for about two hours. Stir occasionally.

4 The chutney is ready when it is thick, has an even consistency and there is no longer any excess liquid.

5 Remove the muslin-wrapped ginger and spoon the chutney into hot canning jars with two-piece lids. Process for 10 minutes in a boiling-water canner. It will be ready to eat after three weeks and will keep for up to three months. Refrigerate after opening.

Chermoula

One of the basic building blocks of taste, providing a complex base flavor for a variety of dishes. Make this up fresh, as and when you need it, to retain the color and pungency. Makes about one cup of paste.

2 Spanish onions

3 cloves garlic

1 bunch flat-leafed parsley

1 $\frac{1}{2}$ bunches fresh cilantro

4 teaspoons chili powder

4 teaspoons cumin powder

4 teaspoons turmeric powder

4 teaspoons sweet paprika

5 teaspoons salt

$\frac{1}{4}$ cup olive oil

juice of 1 lemon

1 Chop the onions and garlic coarsely.

2 Put them and the remaining ingredients into a food processor and process until you have a fine paste. Refrigerate.

Chili jam

Makes about three cups of jam.

4 red onions

2 sweet red peppers

light olive oil

20 small hot chili peppers

1 pound cherry tomatoes

$\frac{1}{2}$ cup light brown sugar

$\frac{2}{3}$ cup Thai fish sauce (*nam plah*)

1 Chop the onions and sweet peppers finely. Put in a pan and barely cover with olive oil.

2 Chop the chilis and add them. Fry until all are golden brown.

3 Chop the tomatoes in half, then add, and cook until dark brown.

4 Add the sugar and fish sauce and process in a food processor.

Red onion jam

Makes about two cups of jam.

1 pound red onions

1 clove garlic

2 fat red chili peppers

$\frac{1}{4}$ pound (1 stick) butter

6 teaspoons balsamic vinegar

1 Chop the onions and garlic finely. Seed and chop the chilis finely. Cook slowly in the butter, with the lid on, for an hour.

2 Stir in the balsamic vinegar and use when cold. Do not keep for more than a couple of days.

Tapenade

Makes almost 1¼ cups of tapenade.

¾ cup stoned black olives

¾ cup capers

3½ ounces canned anchovy fillets in oil

½ fat red chili pepper

6 sprigs fresh rosemary

1 Put the olives, capers, and anchovies (plus the oil from the can) into a blender or food processor. Seed the chili, chop it finely, and add that. Strip the leaves from the rosemary stalks and add them.

2 Process everything together until well chopped and mixed, but still fairly chunky. Beware of going too far – you'll end up with a formless mush.

Sichuan pickled cucumbers
and black shiitake mushrooms

This pickle provides both contrasting textures and a pleasant tang – some would call it fiery, so if you don't warm to chili heat, remove the chilis after they have been fried. Makes almost 1½ cups of pickle.

25 dried shiitake mushrooms

1 pound cucumbers

salt

1 cup peanut oil

2 tablespoons Sichuan peppercorns

10 small hot chili peppers

3-inch piece root ginger

½ cup sugar

¼ cup light soy sauce

¼ cup rice vinegar

1 Put the mushrooms into a bowl of warm water to rehydrate.

2 Peel and seed the cucumbers, cut them into batons diagonally and lengthwise. Salt lightly for 30 minutes to draw out the water.

3 Bring the oil to smoking point in a wok or large frying pan, add the peppercorns and wait until they turn black, then remove with a straining spoon.

4 Reheat the oil and add the chilis; when they go black add the ginger, peeled and shredded finely. It will spit and splutter a good deal.

5 Add the sugar, soy sauce and vinegar, plus the cucumber batons and mushrooms – pat them dry with a kitchen towel first.

6 Stir around for a minute or two to amalgamate the flavors, then transfer to a bowl. Refrigerate for a day or two to mature.

Apple and raisin chutney

Makes about 3¼ pounds of chutney.

I pound cooking apples

2-inch piece root ginger

6 ounces macadamia nuts

2 fat red chili peppers

I pound raisins

2 cloves garlic

I tablespoon sweet paprika

1¾ cups sugar

I tablespoon cayenne pepper

2 cloves

I tablespoon celery salt

1¾ cups cider vinegar

½ cup mirin – sweet cooking saké

1 Peel and core the apples, then chop them finely. Chop the ginger very finely. Roast and chop the macadamia nuts finely. Seed and chop the chilis finely. Mix with the other ingredients thoroughly, cover with plastic wrap and leave in a cool place for 4–5 hours, stirring occasionally. Pack into jars and seal well. Refrigerate for a month before use.

Fish stock

Makes about two quarts.

1½ cups chopped carrots

1 head celery

1½ cups chopped leeks

1½ cups chopped onions

1 head of garlic

2¼ pounds fish trimmings: best are sole trimmings; then any flatfish trimmings; also monkfish bones; heads
are good but every trace of gills must be removed – blood is the enemy of good fish stock

1 bottle white wine – not your best

5 bay leaves

several sprigs each of fresh tarragon, dill and parsley

12 black peppercorns

1 Peel the carrots, then chop them coarsely with the rest of the unpeeled vegetables. Cut the unpeeled garlic into 2 pieces horizontally. Put them all in a large pot, add the wine, the fish, herbs and enough water to barely cover everything.

2 Boil for 10 minutes, skimming off the impurities.

3 Reduce the temperature to a simmer and continue to cook for 40 minutes, skimming occasionally.

4 If your stock is destined for soup, pass it through a sieve and reduce by half to concentrate the flavor.

5 If it is to be used in a sauce, pass through a sieve and use as it is.

Chicken stock

Makes about 9 cups of stock.

1½ cups chopped carrots

1 head celery

1½ cups chopped leeks

1½ cups chopped onions

1 head of garlic

2 chicken carcasses *or* the equivalent in bits and pieces – chicken wings are often the cheapest option

1 bottle white wine – not your best!

5 bay leaves

several sprigs fresh parsley

12 black peppercorns

1 tablespoon sweet paprika

1 Peel the carrots, then chop them coarsely with the rest of the unpeeled vegetables. Slice the unpeeled garlic head in half horizontally. Put everything into a large pot and just cover with water.

2 Bring to a boil for 10 minutes, skimming off the impurities.

3 Reduce the temperature to a simmer and continue to cook for 50 minutes, skimming continually.

4 Pass through a sieve and reduce by a third before use.

Vegetable stock

The Livebait recipe for vegetable stock reflects the fact that there is always an amazing range of fresh vegetables on hand. If you have the time (and the inclination), make this stock according to the recipe at least once – it's interesting to see what an intense and fresh flavor it delivers. Then, when you need a vegetable stock in the future, use it as a starting point and omit any three or four of the components that are unavailable. Makes about 9 cups of stock.

3 leeks

3 carrots

2 stalks celery

2 red onions

1 head garlic

3 plum tomatoes

1 parsnip

1 turnip

1 bunch flat parsley

$\frac{1}{2}$ bunch rosemary

$\frac{1}{2}$ bunch thyme

$\frac{1}{2}$ bunch oregano

$\frac{1}{2}$ bunch chervil

3 bay leaves

6 black peppercorns

11 cups water

1 Clean and chop the leeks, celery, and onions, leaving the skin on. Peel and chop the carrots. Cut the garlic head in half horizontally. Seed and halve the plum tomatoes. Scrub and chop the root vegetables. Chop the herbs coarsely.

2 Put everything into a large pan with the water, bring to a boil, reduce the heat and simmer for 90 minutes.

3 Strain the stock through a sieve, pressing the vegetable residue with a spoon to squeeze out all the juices.

pickles, preserves and sauces

189

Aïoli

If you want it a touch more pungent you can add more garlic. It is still the advice of health agencies that we do not eat raw eggs, which rules out aïoli unless your supermarket stocks those prepacked, pasteurized egg yolks. If you disagree with the official line and wish to take the responsibility on yourself, use really good fresh eggs that are free range and come from a flock certified free of salmonella. Makes about 1¼ cups of aïoli.

4 cloves garlic

salt and black pepper

1 egg yolk

1 cup good olive oil

Working by hand

1 With a mortar and pestle, pound the garlic with a good pinch of salt and some pepper.
2 Add the egg yolk and work in.
3 Add the oil gradually until you have a thick emulsion – like mayonnaise.
4 Adjust the seasoning with salt and pepper.

Using a blender or food processor

1 Put in everything but the oil, and process together.
2 Leave the machine running as you trickle the oil in to produce a thick emulsion.
3 Adjust the seasoning with salt and pepper.

Horseradish cream

This will put you off store-bought horseradish sauce forever. Although nothing is quite like freshly grated horseradish root, the next best thing is the commercial grated horseradish that you sometimes find in jars at smart food shops. Makes about 1 $\frac{1}{4}$ cups.

$\frac{1}{2}$ pound fresh horseradish root (about 1 cup grated)

$\frac{3}{4}$ cup crème fraîche

1 squeeze of lemon juice

1 teaspoon salt

1 Peel the horseradish root with a potato peeler, then grate it into a bowl using the fine side of your grater. Do not inhale deeply – horseradish is fiercely pungent.

2 Add the lemon juice and salt, mix thoroughly. Then add a little crème fraîche and mix in. Continue adding a bit at a time until there's just enough cream to bind the mixture. Treat the project as if you were making coleslaw in miniature.

Foie gras vinaigrette

Makes approximately about one cup of vinaigrette.

4 ounces fresh foie gras *or* tinned *bloc de foie gras*

$\frac{1}{2}$ cup light olive oil

$\frac{1}{4}$ cup balsamic vinegar

6 capers

1 Put the foie gras into a heatproof dish and stand it in a pan of boiling water until it has just firmed up. Take off the stove and allow to cool.

2 Put it with the other ingredients in a food processor and process until all is liquid.

3 Enjoy the self-indulgence, and the richness!

Balsamic vinaigrette

Makes about one cup.

3 tablespoons spicy brown mustard

2 tablespoons honey

$\frac{1}{2}$ cup balsamic vinegar

$\frac{1}{2}$ cup extra virgin olive oil

salt and pepper to taste

▮ Mix together thoroughly by shaking in a screw-topped jar.

Hot chili vinaigrette

Makes about one cup.

3 tablespoons spicy brown mustard

I tablespoon hot chili paste

2 tablespoons honey

$\frac{1}{2}$ cup red wine vinegar

$\frac{1}{2}$ cup extra virgin olive oil

salt to taste

▮ Mix together thoroughly by shaking in a screw-topped jar. Beware – hot!

Pernod sauce

An amazing sauce. So simple. So delicious. So try it! Makes about ⅔ cup of sauce.

⅔ cup Pernod

4 tablespoons cold butter

salt and pepper

1 Heat a stainless steel pan, pour in the Pernod and allow to bubble.

2 Cut the butter (which must be chilled – straight from the refrigerator) into small cubes.

3 When the Pernod has reduced by a third, whisk in the butter a little at a time. The sauce will thicken and "polish" up, becoming glossy.

4 Taste the sauce and adjust the seasoning.

Sauce gribiche

Makes about ¾ cup of sauce.

½ cup olive oil

2 tablespoons red wine vinegar

¼ cup smooth Dijon mustard

2 hard-boiled eggs

⅓ cup cornichons

⅓ cup capers

salt and pepper

1 Mix the oil and vinegar in a bowl, and stir in the mustard.

2 Finely chop the hard-boiled eggs and add them. Coarsely chop the cornichons and add them.

3 Stir in the capers, then adjust the seasoning.

Sauce choron

Makes about ¾ cup of sauce.

2 shallots

⅔ cup white wine

¼ cup tarragon vinegar

1 tablespoon fresh tarragon

8 peppercorns

3 egg yolks

1 tablespoon Colman's mustard powder

1 tablespoon tomato purée

2 tablespoons soft butter

½ pound (2 sticks) melted butter

salt

juice of ½ lemon

1 plum tomato

1 Chop the shallots very finely and put them with the wine, tarragon vinegar, fresh tarragon and peppercorns into a pan and heat until bubbling. Cook until reduced by a third.

2 Whisk the egg yolks and mustard in a large bowl – the right size to sit easily over a saucepan of hot water during the next stage.

3 Stir the tomato purée into the vinegar mixture, allow to cool and strain through a fine sieve on to the egg yolks.

4 Take a whisk and beat the egg yolk mixture over a pan of hot water. (You seek to keep the sauce warm but never too hot or the eggs will scramble.) It will help if you start by whisking in a little (2 tablespoons) lukewarm water. Then whisk in the soft butter a little at a time until the sauce is thick and glossy.

5 Now add the melted butter – a little at a time – whisking as you go. Finally, season with salt and lemon juice to taste. Peel, seed, and dice the tomato finely; stir it in. Keep the sauce warm over hot water until it's needed.

Gazpacho sauce

Makes about ¾ cup of sauce.

5 large plum tomatoes

1 clove garlic

1 small red onion

3 tablespoons breadcrumbs

2 tablespoons plus 2 teaspoons good olive oil

1 tablespoon sherry vinegar

salt and pepper

1 Preheat your oven to 400°F.

2 Cut the tomatoes in half and roast on a baking tray in the oven for 15 minutes.

3 Peel and chop the garlic and onion, and place them with the other ingredients in a blender and process until liquidized.

4 Pass the sauce through a sieve.

5 Adjust seasoning.

Vanilla pod sauce

Makes about ⅔ cup.

6 vanilla pods

2 shallots

¾ cup white wine

⅔ cup water

juice of ½ lemon

6 tablespoons heavy cream

zest of 1 lemon

1 Split the vanilla pods lengthwise and strip the tiny seeds into a pan.

2 Add the pods, shallots, wine, water and lemon juice.

3 Heat until bubbling, then cook until reduced by two thirds.

4 Remove from the heat and leave to infuse for 10 minutes, then remove the pieces of vanilla pod and whisk in the cream and lemon zest. Warm through gently, but do not allow to boil or the sauce will split.

5 Season with a little salt.

Cumin sauce

Makes about ⅔ cup of sauce.

2 teaspoons cumin seeds

2 Spanish onions

1 clove garlic

2 tablespoons olive oil

1¼ cups Fish Stock (see page 186)

1¼ cups white wine

¼ pound (1 stick) cold, unsalted butter

salt and pepper

1 Toast the cumin seeds in a dry pan, and reserve.

2 Finely chop the onions; peel and crush the garlic. Soften them both in a little oil in a frying pan.

3 Add the cumin and the fish stock, then reduce by half.

4 Add the wine and reduce by two-thirds so that you end up with ⅔ cup of liquid.

5 Pass through a sieve into a clean pan, bring to a boil and whisk in the chilled butter straight from the fridge, cut into cubes, a little at a time – this will give a glossy, thickened sauce. Adjust seasoning to taste.

Celeriac remoulade

If you make the sauce first, and then grate the celeriac into it, you avoid having to keep the celeriac in acidulated water to stop it darkening. Makes over a pound.

$^2/_3$ cup crème fraîche

2 tablespoons Dijon mustard

juice of 1 lemon

2 tablespoons pickled green peppercorns

salt

$^3/_4$-pound piece celeriac root

sweet paprika

1 Mix the crème fraîche with the mustard and lemon juice, stir in the peppercorns and season to taste with salt.

2 Peel the celeriac and shred it as finely as you are able; as you go, fold it into the crème fraîche mixture.

3 When serving, sprinkle a pinch of paprika over the top.

Baba ganoush

This eggplant "paste," is a good source of taste and an instant marinade – very useful. Makes about 1$^1/_4$ cups.

2 large eggplants

2 cloves garlic

3 tablespoons tahini paste

juice of $^1/_2$ lemon

1 tablespoon cumin powder

salt to taste

1 Cook the eggplants under a broiler, or by turning them over a naked flame on a fork until they are black, then place them in a plastic bag and put to one side.

2 When they are cold, simply rub off the skins with your fingers, peeling any stubborn patches with a knife. Squeeze out the bitter juices – again by hand.

3 Put all the ingredients into a blender or food processor and process until very smooth. Add salt to taste and process again to mix. Allow to stand for at least an hour before use.

Red pepper coulis

Although it may be used fresh, the flavors will amalgamate and the coulis will improve if kept for a day in the refrigerator. Makes about two cups of coulis.

3 red peppers

3 plum tomatoes

2 fat red chili peppers

1 red onion

$\frac{1}{4}$ cup olive oil

1 cup plus 2 tablespoons of Chicken Stock (see page 188) or water

scant $\frac{1}{2}$ cup red wine

2 star anise

$\frac{1}{4}$ cup grenadine syrup

salt and pepper

1 Preheat your oven to 350°F.

2 Seed and quarter the peppers, and put them in a roasting pan with the tomatoes and chilis. Peel and quarter the red onion and add. Brush with oil and roast for 20 minutes.

3 Put the roasted vegetables, the chicken stock, the wine and the star anise into a saucepan, bring to a boil and cook fiercely until the liquid is reduced by three-quarters.

4 Remove the star anise and purée everything else in a blender or food processor until very smooth. Pass the coulis through a strainer, stir in the grenadine syrup, and adjust the seasoning with salt and pepper.

Simple pasta dough

The basic rule of thumb for pasta is that every diner should get an egg and 4 ounces of flour! Thus the only variables are how much water and salt to add. The former is governed by the feel of the dough in your hands and the latter by your taste buds (aided by trial and error). This recipe serves four.

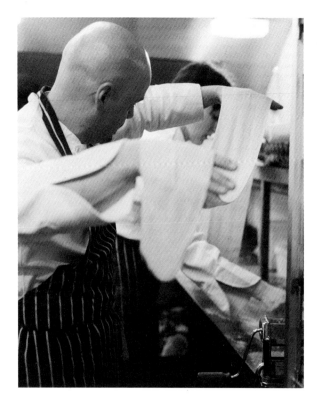

1 pound Italian pasta flour

4 medium eggs

1 heaped teaspoon salt

1 If you have a pasta machine, follow the directions that come with it.

2 Heap the flour on your work surface and make a central well. Then whisk the eggs with the salt and pour into the well. Use a fork to bring the flour into the middle and as soon as possible switch to kneading by hand.

3 Knead for 5 minutes, then rest the dough, covered in plastic wrap, for 30 minutes.

4 Back to the dough, and knead for another 5 minutes. By now it should feel heavy, smooth and stretchy.

5 Take your longest rolling pin. After flouring it, and the work surface, roll out the dough into a circle. Try to work away from yourself and rotate the piece of dough as you do so. For ravioli, roll out the dough as thinly as possible.

Lentil stew

Serves four.

½ cup chopped shallots

2 cloves garlic

⅓ cup olive oil

1⅔ cups lentils

2 bay leaves

3 cups Chicken Stock (see page 188)

salt and pepper

some good olive oil

some balsamic vinegar

1 Finely chop the shallots, crush the garlic, and cook them both with the olive oil in a heavy saucepan. Do not let them go soft. While they are still crunchy, add the lentils, bay leaves, and the chicken stock. Cover the pan, and simmer as slowly as possible until cooked – between 40 and 60 minutes. Do not overcook as the lentils will turn to mush. Do not season at all during cooking as salt hardens lentils.

2 To finish the lentils, simply season with salt and pepper and stir in a splash of good olive oil and some balsamic vinegar.

Shopping and showing off

This is a simple dish, and any green or brown lentils will suffice. If you cannot find shallots, substitute mild onions.

Home-cured mackerel

Serves eight.

4 mackerel, each 12 ounces

1 fat red chili pepper

2 cups granulated sugar

1 cup sea salt

12 tarragon leaves

6 juniper berries

1 Ask your fishmonger to fillet the mackerel and remove the pin bones.

2 Chop the chili finely, and add it to the sugar, salt, tarragon and juniper. Mix thoroughly.

3 Put a layer of the mixture in a plastic container and add the fish fillets skin side down.

4 Top with another layer of the mixture, then more fillets, ending with a layer of mixture.

5 Keep covered in a refrigerator (not too cold!) for 48 hours. The salt mixture will turn to liquid. At the end of the first day turn the fillets over.

6 Before use, rinse the fish well.

Potato, cilantro and lemongrass dauphinoise

A novel take on the classic dauphinoise. Serves four.

1 clove garlic

2 tablespoons butter

$2\frac{1}{4}$ pounds potatoes

1 bunch fresh cilantro

6 ounces lemongrass

2 cups whole milk

4 ounces soft cow's milk cheese

$\frac{2}{3}$ cup crème fraîche

salt and pepper

1 Preheat your oven to 350°F.

2 Use a large flat gratin dish so that the potato mixture is less than $1\frac{1}{4}$ inches deep. Cut the garlic clove in half and rub the dish all over with the cut end. Then butter the dish.

3 Peel the potatoes and slice them very thinly; rinse them in fresh water to get rid of surface starch.

4 Strip the leaves from the cilantro and chop finely. Peel the lemongrass back to the tender middle and chop it very finely.

5 Bring the milk up to a boil in a saucepan. Remove from the heat and stir in the cheese, crème fraîche, cilantro, and lemongrass. Then add the potatoes and stir in. Season with salt and pepper.

6 Spoon the contents into the gratin dish, spreading it out evenly into a layer no more than $1\frac{1}{4}$ inches thick.

7 Bake in the oven for 80–90 minutes. Brown under the broiler to finish, if necessary.

Shopping and showing off

At Livebait, we use an English cheese called Wellington for this dish, but any soft cow's milk cheese will add the required richness.

Index

index